W9-BFI-002

COFFEE COOKERY

by Ceil Dyer

ANOTHER BEST-SELLING COOKERY VOLUME FROM H.P. BOOKS

Author: Ceil Dyer; Publisher: Helen Fisher; Editor: Carlene Tejada; Senior Editor: Jon Latimer; Editor-in-Chief: Carl Shipman; Art Director: Don Burton; Book Design & Assembly: Laura Hardock; Typography: Connie Brown, Cindy Coatsworth; Research Assistant: Mrs. Gafford Pearce; Food Stylist: Mable Hoffman; Photography: George deGennaro Studios. Special thanks to Sr. Helio Guerreiro of the Brazilian Coffee Institute for his cooperation.

Published by H.P. Books, P. O. Box 5367, Tucson, AZ 85703 602/888-2150

ISBN: Softcover, 0-89586-009-0; Hardcover, 0-89586-010-4
Library of Congress Catalog Card Number, 78-61888
©1978 Fisher Publishing, Inc.
Printed in U.S.A.

Cover Photo: Java Spice Cake, page 93

The Fascination of Coffee

Coffee! What would life be like without a steaming cup? Around the world people fashion their lifestyles around this fragrant brew.

In France the morning begins with steamy hot *café au lait*. Business meetings and romances begin over small cups of black coffee in Parisian cafés. Tahitian housewives offer tall glasses of supersweet coffee as a welcoming gesture. African merchants serve it to every customer before the bargaining begins. And in Vienna, afternoon coffee is an established part of the day. For the Viennese to abandon their coffee, generously topped with dollops of thick rich whipped cream, would be unthinkable. The Dutch, Germans, Turks, Arabs, and South Americans are all coffee enthusiasts.

Since revolutionary days when the new Americans switched from taxed English tea to coffee, it has been the national beverage of the United States.

Coffee grew in Abyssinia before Christian times but the Arabs were the first to cultivate it and use it as a beverage. Today, the largest part of the world's supply of coffee comes from South America, but strangely enough, its ancestors were Dutch and French. In 1813 the Dutch presented a coffee tree to the King of France. In 1723, seeds from this tree were carried to Martinique by a young French officer. And so began the legendary coffee plantations of the western world.

Although modern times have improved cultivation and production, coffee still must be picked and sorted by hand. Over 2,000 coffee *berries* must be handpicked to make 1 pound of roasted coffee. It's a labor of love and expertise and a reason why coffee deserves to be handled with care and respect.

But the real fascination of coffee is its flavor. Nothing else has the tantilizing aroma or the rich flavor of freshly prepared coffee. That's why this book begins with the how-to's of perfect coffee: how to buy it, how to store it and how to brew it. Follow the directions and you can serve one great cup of coffee after another, time after time.

Because the flavor of coffee is so magical and appeals to so many people, I have not stopped with just a cup of coffee. You'll also find recipes in this book using coffee as an ingredient. Coffee adds its unique flavor to satin-smooth custards, sinfully rich puddings, elegant soufflés and frozen de-

lights—all guaranteed to enhance your reputation as an inspired cook. Then there are the coffee candies, cookies and an assortment of subtly flavored sauces to transform simple ice cream and plain custards into glamorous desserts. You'll enjoy my collection of main course non-sweet dishes flavored very subtly with coffee. You won't taste the coffee, but you'll notice the enhanced flavor of the dish.

As you've already guessed, I love coffee, but who doesn't? Coffee brewing and coffee cookery are fun things to do and the more ways you can find to use coffee, the more fun it is. That's the fascination of coffee for me. I hope you'll find the same fun and fascination as you use this book.

Now it's time for a break to brew coffee. Won't you join me?

Coffee Grinders

Grinding your own coffee beans will give you a fresher brew. A number of different types of coffee grinders are available. Electric grinders range in capacity from 4 cups, as in the one shown above, to over a pound. Some use a spinning blade for grinding while others use a drill-like burr. Most work quickly and efficiently. Some are much quieter than others and you should check before you buy.

There are also a number of different types of hand mills, including antique models which are more for show than use. Different types have different capacities. They can be secured to a wall or clamped to a counter or table top. Most can be adjusted to grind as coarse or fine as you prefer.

HOW TO MAKE PERFECT COFFEE— CUP AFTER CUP

The key to perfect coffee is *freshness.* Always use fresh coffee, pure fresh water and a clean, fresh-smelling coffeemaker. Whatever method you use to make coffee, these 3 rules give perfect coffee time after time:

1. **Start with fresh water.** It's 99.8% of the brew. Water that stands in the pipes several hours or over-night takes on a subtle but unpleasant taste. No matter how rushed or how sleepy you are or how intense your early morning blur, turn on the cold water tap and let the water flow until it runs cold and fresh. If there is a water shortage in your area, you can catch the first running in a large pitcher to keep for other uses.

2. **Buy only fresh coffee.** Roasted coffee beans, once exposed to light and air, lose their fresh flavor and aroma within a few hours. This loss begins within minutes after the coffee beans are ground. Coffee connoisseurs will tell you that the best way to obtain truly fresh coffee and peak-flavor brew is to buy only the finest, freshly roasted beans—and never more than a few days supply—rush home, transfer the beans to an airtight container and store the container in the freezer; then, just before making coffee, grind only what you need for a single pot.

This is not the only way to a perfect cup of coffee. Although I enjoy shopping for special blends of freshly roasted beans and grinding them myself— my electric coffee grinder has been well worth the price—it's not the only way to obtain fresh-roasted flavor. Far from it. I have found that the top quality, vacuum-packed, ground coffee is as flavorful and fresh when first opened as the bean coffee I grind at home.

Unless you have access to a market where you can buy a really good blend of freshly roasted coffee beans, vacuum-packed, ground coffee is your best choice. Reputable food companies make every effort to get freshly roasted and ground coffee beans under vacuum seal as fast as the most modern methods allow. Sealed in, the flavor will last, not forever, but until it reaches you. That whiff of fragrance when you first open the coffee can is the smell of fresh-ground coffee. After the can is opened, cover it with its own snap-on lid and store it in the freezer. For a week to 10 days it will remain as fresh as when it was first opened.

3. **Use a fresh-smelling coffeemaker.** Regardless of the type you prefer, automatic, drip percolator, imported or domestic, keep your coffeemaker clean! For a cloudless, fresh-tasting, robust—but not bitter—brew, it's necessary to scrub the coffee-maker thoroughly after each use, then rinse it well and set it to dry in the open air. If you use a perc-olator, don't forget to clean the spout too. Coffee leaves an oily residue that cannot be rinsed away even with the hottest of water. It must be scrubbed with soapy water. If this oily residue remains in the pot, it will build up and become rancid. Then all your efforts for fresh-tasting, fragrant coffee will be wasted. Don't let this happen to you!

Ceil Dyer

Ceil Dyer's flair for combining ingredients to create a delicious dish reflects her thrifty upbringing and intimate knowledge of a variety of cuisines and cultures. As a food editor and publicist for several large companies, Ceil traveled through Europe learning everything she could about its cooking, wines and cultures. For a number of years she wrote a syndicated column, "The Instant Gourmet." Then she added one cookbook success after another, in-cluding THE CARTER FAMILY COOKBOOK. HPBooks fans know her for the popular WOK COOKERY.

Beans, Blends & Basics

When you buy coffee in the supermarket, the label tells you nothing about the origin or type of coffee bean used. Basically there are 2 varieties of coffee: *robusta* and *arabica.*

The robusta variety is grown at lower altitudes than the arabica. It's cheaper, contains larger amounts of caffeine and has a more bitter flavor. Vacuum-packed coffees, instant coffee powders and freeze-dried coffees are usually made from blends of various robustas.

The more flavorful arabicas are cultivated on high mountain sides and are not as plentiful as the robustas. Therefore they are more expensive. These are the beans and freshly ground coffees you can buy in gourmet and specialty shops. Although connoisseurs consider mountain-grown coffee to be much better quality than the lower-grown robustas, and coffees from specific high regions have more gourmet appeal than others, the quality of the beans can vary from year to year in the same region.

THE COFFEE HARVEST

Coffee is one of the world's abundant crops. It is produced in more than 30 countries. Only a few of the coffees produced for world consumption are mentioned here.

Brazil grows the basic beans for many of the world's coffee blends. They range from the mild, light flavor of *Santos* beans to *Rio* coffee used in cheaper blends.

The Colombian *Supremo* has more flavor and fragrance than the Santos. *Excelso,* a blend of Supremo and Colombia's lower grade *Extra* beans, is imported to the United States in greater quantities than any other coffee.

Guatemala's *Antigua* beans are the best known of the Central American coffees. However, delightful and aromatic blends can be made from a mixture of Central American coffees. Nicaragua, Costa Rica and El Salvador all grow fine aromatic coffee beans.

Most coffee drinkers find *Kona* coffee from Hawaii delicious and satisfying. It also blends well with most other coffees.

Mocha Java is a highly regarded blend. The *Mocha* is grown in Yemen or Ethiopia and the *Java* is the arabica variety from Indonesia.

Probably the most highly prized coffee of all is *Blue Mountain* coffee, produced in Jamaica. This is an extremely rare coffee, available only in limited quantities. It is, of course, very expensive.

Once the coffee beans have been grown and harvested, the 3 most important factors influencing coffee flavor are roasting, blending and grinding.

ROASTS

Roasting coffee beans lowers the acid and caffein contents of the coffee and gives it a sweeter taste with more flavor. Roasting also masks the individual characteristics which make one coffee different from another. The darker the roast, the less unique the flavor of the coffee. All the more reason, say the roasters, for using the inferior, less unique bean for a dark roast.

Standard roasts are usually done to a medium brown and are mildly flavored. Slightly darker and sweeter are *Vienna roast* and *espresso roast.* Darkest of all are the *French roast* and *dark French* or *Italian roast.* Try blending one of the darker roast beans with a standard roast. You'll find you can vary the flavor of the blends by mixing the different degrees of roast as well as the type of bean.

Roasting coffee beans brings out their oil. This is why it's important to obtain fresh coffee and store it in the refrigerator or buy coffee that has been vacuum-packed and use it within a short time. Not only will coffee lose its flavor but it can become rancid if precautions aren't taken to preserve freshness.

BLENDS

Supermarket coffee is a blend of fine coffee beans and inferior filler or robusta beans. If you want to choose the beans that go into the blend, ask the coffee person at your local gourmet shop to make an extra-special blend for you. A popular blend to start you on the way to making up your own is equal parts Java, Mocha and Excelso. You may prefer Hawaii's Kona in place of the Java.

If the blend you end up with contains a large amount of Colombian or Hawaiian coffee, you may find it has a lighter body that you like. If this is the case, the next time you choose your own blend, add some full-flavored, highly aromatic Sumatran, Kenyan or Tanzanian beans.

Keep in mind that coffee beans from Kenya and Hawaii blend well with most good mild coffees. Chicory, used by many people as a coffee substitute, can impart new and delicious flavor to your own private blend.

Listen to suggestions from the coffee authority at the local specialty shop, but don't be afraid to use your own instincts and sniffing abilities. After all, you alone know how you want your coffee to taste.

GRINDS

Loss of flavor begins as soon as the beans are ground. And the finer the grind, the more flavor is lost. If ground coffee is vacuum-packed, refrigerated and used within a week or 10 days, most of us won't notice the loss of flavor. However, if you grind your own coffee, use it within the week. If you keep it longer, you will probably notice the flavor difference.

Each method of brewing coffee requires its own type of grind. Be sure you are using the appropriate one. If your coffee is ground too fine for the method you are using, the coffee will taste bitter and contain a lot of sediment. If the beans are ground too coarsely, the coffee will turn out weak.

HOW TO BUY COFFEE

If you buy coffee beans, buy from a coffee merchant who roasts his beans in small quantities each day. If this isn't possible, buy from a large supermarket chain store. They sell coffee beans in such volume that they have little time to become stale.

Don't buy so-called gourmet bean coffee packaged in fancy labeled paper bags from a small shop that stocks it only as a sideline. More often than not it will become stale waiting for a customer.

If you buy ground coffee, buy it in vacuum-packed cans—not packaged in paper bags. Paper can't protect the grounds from air and the loss of flavor and aroma isn't worth the pennies saved.

HOW TO MEASURE

Measure coffee and water accurately. It's the only way to achieve consistent results. For full-bodied but not overstrong coffee, use 2 level tablespoons of coffee grounds to each 3/4 cup of water. This applies to any grind of coffee or any type coffeemaker. An exception is very fine ground coffee used in making such coffees as espresso or Turkish. These are usually made in special pots. Follow the manufacturer's instructions, then adjust the measurements to your own taste.

American Coffee

Cappucino

Neither the type of coffee used nor the length of preparation time influences the *strength* of the brew. It is the amount of coffee and the type of grind that is most important in developing the brew's strength.

HOW TO USE YOUR COFFEEMAKER

Don't use chemically softened or very hard water to brew coffee. If the water in your area is highly chlorinated, sulphurous or tastes of other chemicals, buy bottled spring water. You'll find it worth the few cents per pot in the resulting coffee enjoyment.

Be sure to use the right grind of coffee for your particular coffeemaker. The wrong grind can result in coffee that's too strong or too weak.

Don't attempt to make less than 3/4 the capacity of your coffeemaker. The results won't be satisfactory. The exception is the new electric coffeemakers that let you select the amount of coffee you want to make.

Time your coffeemaker. Vacuum and espresso pots using very fine or powdered coffee should take no more than 1 to 3 minutes. Drip pots using finely ground coffee require no more than 4 minutes. Percolator pots using an all-purpose grind usually need no more than 6 minutes. More than 6 to 8 minutes by any other method will cause over-extraction and produce only bitter, not strong, coffee.

For pure, clear, full-flavor coffee with no sediment, select a coffeemaker that uses a filter paper. It will make good coffee better, fine coffee superb.

Don't let coffee boil, ever! Boiling brings out tannic acid and makes coffee evil-tasting.

HOW TO SERVE COFFEE

Serve coffee as soon as possible after brewing. If necessary, keep it hot on an asbestos pad over low heat, or on the warm setting of your electric coffeemaker, or in a pan of hot water or by whatever method required for your particular pot.

To keep coffee from cooling when it's poured into your carafe or best china pot, rinse out the cold carafe or pot with very hot water just before filling with coffee. If you're making instant coffee in a carafe or pot, rinse the carafe or pot with hot water, measure in the needed amounts of instant coffee powder and almost boiling water. Stir and serve immediately.

Caffè Espresso

Demitasse au Café

HOW TO MAKE INSTANT COFFEE

Although I will go to any lengths time and money will allow to obtain a perfect cup of freshly brewed coffee, there comes an extra-busy morning or what I call the "4 o'clock collapse" when out comes the jar of *instant*.

There's no doubt about it. The top makers of instant coffee have given us a great product. Instant coffee is convenient to have on hand, double-quick to prepare and is, so the experts tell us, less expensive cup for cup than brewed coffee. Although coffee lovers insist nothing matches the flavor of freshly brewed coffee—and I agree—instant coffee has its well-earned place on my kitchen shelf, as I'm sure it does on yours.

Like any other good thing, a little care in the making pays off in total enjoyment. Start with fresh cold water. Bring it to a full boil then remove it from the heat. When the boiling subsides, pour the water over the carefully measured instant coffee powder. Rapidly boiling water tends to make instant coffee bitter. Careless measuring usually results in either too weak or too strong coffee. One level teaspoon to each 8-ounce cup of water makes the perfect strength for most tastes.

Here are some hints to boost instant coffee a notch in flavor:

● Add 1/2 teaspoon grated semisweet chocolate to each teaspoon of instant coffee before adding water.
● Drop a thin twist of lemon peel in each cup of instant espresso coffee and pass a dish of tiny dot cubes of sugar.
● Pour half just-made instant coffee and half hot milk into thick mugs and sweeten with light brown sugar.
● Use specially flavored sugars—you'll find 3 easy recipes on page 23.
● Try any of the above then add a splash of brandy or orange liqueur to each cup.

COFFEE AS AN INGREDIENT

What type coffee should you use when a recipe calls for coffee? It depends on your preference and the recipe.

When pure coffee flavor is suspended in gelatin as in a clear coffee gelatin dessert, I prefer to use freshly brewed coffee from freshly roasted and ground beans.

Can you use leftover coffee? Yes, you can. That's part of the fun of cooking with coffee. It's a superb flavoring costing nothing if it uses coffee that

Turkish Coffee

Café au Lait

would otherwise be poured down the drain. When the recipe specifies hot coffee, it's best to keep left-over coffee hot and use it as soon as possible. If coffee is reheated or held too long over heat, it tends to develop an acid taste. If it's not possible to keep coffee hot, store it in the refrigerator. This helps keep it fresh. When you're ready to use it, bring the coffee to room temperature and slowly reheat.

Instant coffee is, in my opinion, the best ingredient coffee for many recipes—especially when I want strong coffee flavor but the recipe calls for little or no liquid. When dry, right-from-the-jar instant coffee is called for, I prefer the powdered variety. It dissolves faster and mixes more easily with other ingredients than freeze-dried granular coffee. If you have only freeze-dried granular coffee on hand, you can easily crush it yourself for the same quick-dissolving and easy-mixing results. Place the granules in a sturdy plastic bag and crush with a mallet or rolling pin. You can also crush them in your blender.

If you like strong coffee flavor but want to use your rather mild leftover coffee from breakfast, stir in a teaspoon or more of instant coffee. Or make extra-strong fresh coffee. It will probably be too bitter to drink, but the bitterness will be lost by blending with the other flavors in the recipe.

Three forms of coffee are mentioned in the recipes in this book: instant coffee powder, prepared coffee and ground coffee. When a recipe calls for 1 cup of prepared coffee, use leftover black coffee or just-made coffee. The recipe will indicate if it's necessary for the coffee to be either hot or cold. Otherwise the temperature of the coffee is not important.

How To Serve Coffees from Around the World

American Coffee

Whatever method you use, don't boil it. Many people prefer this coffee black, with nothing added, but sugar and cream or milk are always offered. See photo, page 5. To vary your coffee, add a spoonful of Viennese Sugar, Espresso Sugar or Spiced Sugar. You'll find recipes for them on page 23.

Café au Lait

One of the pleasures of breakfasting in France is this warming drink of half very hot milk and half fresh hot strong coffee. The coffee is made in a drip pot using dark roast, finely ground beans. You'll need 2 pots of equal size; one for the coffee and another for the hot milk. Pour simultaneously from both pots into warm cups and sweeten to taste with light brown sugar. See photo, page 7.

Caffè Espresso

To be authentic, this coffee must be made in a steam pressure machine. But acceptable instant espresso coffees and espresso pots are available. Serve espresso in small cups without cream or milk. Twist a thin slice of lemon peel over the cup to release the lemony essence into the hot coffee. Then drop in the lemon peel. Add sugar to taste. See photo, page 6. Italian coffee is similar to espresso except it's made in a Neapolitan or other drip pot. Follow the directions for serving Caffè Espresso.

Cappucino

The real thing is made with espresso coffee in an espresso machine that also heats and froths the milk. The coffee-milk mixture is sweetened to taste and lightly sprinkled with cinnamon. You can make an acceptable likeness using half hot milk and half coffee made in a Neapolitan or other drip pot. You can also use instant espresso. Top the coffee-milk mixture with Sweetened Whipped Cream, page 122, and a sprinkle of cinnamon. See photo, page 5.

Demitasse au Café

Freshly made, hot strong coffee served in small cups called demitasse cups is an elegant after-dinner tradition. Although cream or milk are never added, you may sweeten the coffee to taste with small cubes of sugar. If you like, add a dash of brandy, orange liqueur, white crème de menthe or other compatible liqueur. See photo, page 6.

Turkish Coffee

The tall, long-handled tapering brass or copper pot is called an *ibrik*. Make pulverized coffee by crushing freshly ground coffee beans between wax paper with a rolling pin. Use about 1 tablespoon each of coffee and sugar for each serving. Place in the pot with a cup of water for each serving and bring to a full boil. Remove from the heat until boiling subsides. Repeat the boiling procedure 3 times. Spoon a small amount of the surface foam into each cup, then slowly pour in the unstrained coffee, filling the cups to the brim. See photo, page 7.

Guide To Coffeemakers

Which coffeemakers are right for you? There is an almost limitless variety on the market. Your choice depends on your preferences and needs. If you enjoy coffee as much as I do, you'll probably want a good-size coffeemaker to use at mealtimes and a smaller pot to brew an extra cup or two for a midmorning or afternoon break. You may also want to treat your family and friends to the special taste of espresso coffee.

I hope this guide will help you select the right coffeemakers for your own use and for gifts.

Whichever you choose, make your coffee with care and enjoy the best of all beverages—a steaming cup of fragrant coffee!

Automatic Percolators

Percolators are available in a wide variety of shapes and sizes. Water heated at the bottom of the pot is forced up a central tube into a basket filled with ground coffee. It seeps through the grounds and drops into the heated water. This process is repeated until the heat is turned off.

Electric units have a thermostat that shuts off the heating element when the coffee reaches the desired strength. A warming element then keeps the coffee warm. Grounds should be removed immediately after perking to avoid bitterness. Some experts say percolators do not make very good coffee, but ease of operation has made them by far the most popular coffeemaker. Capacity varies from 2 to 50 cups or more.

Guide To Coffeemakers

Non-Automatic Percolators

These coffeemakers work on the same principle as automatic percolators except that they do not turn themselves off automatically and they require an external heat source such as the burner on your kitchen stove. Non-automatics should be watched to prevent boiling over. You control the strength of the coffee by how long you let it percolate. Non-automatic percolators are inexpensive and available in a wide variety of sizes and styles.

Automatic Drip Makers

These machines have recently become very popular. Coffee grounds are placed in a cone lined with filter paper which rests above the glass decanter. Water is placed in a reservoir where it is heated. The heated water drips over the coffee and into the decanter. The heat turns off automatically—or in some models you must turn it off with a switch. The coffee is kept warm by a separate warming element beneath the decanter. The coffee stays warm and fresh for long periods. Different machines are available with different features. They make rich coffee with a minimum of sediment. Replacement filter papers are available. Most of these make about eight 5-ounce cups of coffee.

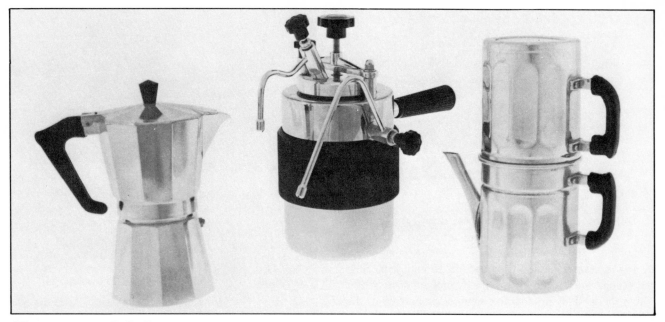

Espresso Makers

Espresso is a very thick, rich brew and is made in small quantities. It normally has some sediment. There is great variety among the different types of makers and some appear very complicated. In the maker shown at left, water is put in the bottom and coffee grounds are placed in the basket in the middle. Placed over heat, the water becomes hot and rises up over the coffee-filled basket until the pot is removed from heat.

The type at right, known as a Neapolitan filter pot, is turned upside down to heat. Water is placed in the half with only a handle. Grounds are placed in a basket between the two pots. The pot with both handle and pouring spout is placed on top, empty. After the water is heated, the entire unit is inverted to the position shown in the photo. Water flows from top to bottom, passing through the grounds. Remove the boiler and basket with grounds, and serve the coffee.

Steam-type espresso makers, one of which is shown in the center, heat water in a sealed boiler and then force it through coffee grounds held in a metal filter. The model shown is heated on a stove, but some have built-in electric heating elements.

Filter Cone Method

This simple coffeemaker has a cone at the top which holds a folded piece of filter paper filled with finely ground coffee. You pour water that is almost boiling into the cone where it drips through the coffee and collects in the bottom of the pot. The water picks up the flavor and color of coffee, but leaves behind the bitterness and sediment. Grounds can then be lifted out with the filter paper and thrown away. Some one-piece types have a wooden collar as a handle, others are in two pieces. Some models are available with a warming unit to keep the coffee at serving temperature. Replacement filters cost a few pennies each. Capacity varies from 1 to 12 cups.

Guide To Coffeemakers

French Plunger Pots

This type of coffeemaker produces strong, thick coffee in a short time. A measured amount of coffee is placed in the cylinder and water that is barely boiling is poured over it. The mixture is allowed to steep for 3 or 4 minutes. Then the plunger in the top of the pot is pressed down which forces the grounds through the brew to the bottom of the pot. The filter on the plunger traps the grounds and holds them at the bottom. Very little sediment escapes into the coffee. These usually make 6 to 8 cups of coffee but other sizes are available.

Cold Water Method

This method produces a rich syrupy coffee concentrate which is then mixed with boiling water to make coffee for drinking. One pound of coffee is placed into the canister and 8 cups of cold water are added. The mixture is allowed to sit overnight. The canister is then placed over the glass bottle and the coffee concentrate drips into it. This may take an hour or more. The concentrate collected in the bottle should be refrigerated for future use. Coffee produced by this method is rich and full-bodied, and is made as quickly as instant from the concentrate. There is little of the bitterness that is released by high-temperature brewing, and no sediment. The concentrate makes as many as 40 cups of coffee.

Coffee Specials

Coffee's unique and irresistible flavor blends into an endless variety of hot and cold drinks. All the drinks in this section are quick to make but each one has a different appeal. Serve Cinnamon Cafe con Leche in front of the fireplace on a cold winter day. Sip Coffee-Mint Soda through a straw when you're feeling gay and lighthearted. Mochachino—rich with cocoa, cinnamon and marshmallows—is a teenage favorite. Peachy Frosteds are great summer refreshers.

If you can't make up your mind, give a coffee party so you and your friends can try them all. Assemble the ingredients for the drinks you want to try. Have a pot of fresh hot coffee ready and your blender on hand. Arrange everything on a big tray with mugs, cups and glasses. As soon as the guests arrive, start whipping up drinks to order, soda-shoppe style. A platter of sandwiches makes it a supper party. End the evening with a tray of coffee cookies, pages 132 to 148.

A Very Special Luncheon

Chicken Montego in Patty Shells, page 31
Steamed Broccoli
Walnut Squares With Apricot
Sauce, page 105
Iced Coffee Continental, page 15

Spiced Coffee

Spicy hot coffee swirled with coffee-flavored whipped cream.

Coffee Whipped Cream, see below
3-1/2 cups water
2 (1-inch) cinnamon sticks,
    broken in small pieces

10 to 12 whole cloves
6 to 8 whole allspice berries
4 teaspoons instant coffee powder,
    more if desired

Coffee Whipped Cream:
1/2 cup whipping cream
2 tablespoons sugar

1 tablespoon instant coffee powder

Prepare Coffee Whipped Cream. Refrigerate. In a medium saucepan, combine water, cinnamon sticks, cloves and allspice berries. Bring to a boil. Reduce heat and simmer 10 minutes. Place 1 teaspoon instant coffee powder in each of 4 coffee mugs. Use more instant coffee powder if stronger coffee is desired. With a small strainer, strain spiced water into mugs, filling mugs 3/4 full. Stir. Top with Coffee Whipped Cream and serve immediately. Makes 4 servings.

Coffee Whipped Cream:
In a small bowl, mix cream, sugar and instant coffee powder. Chill. Beat until stiff.

Mochachino

A chocolate-coffee blend topped with marshmallows.

2 tablespoons instant coffee powder
2 (1-oz.) envelopes cocoa mix
1/4 teaspoon cinnamon

1/2 cup almost boiling water
2 cups milk
Marshmallows

Place instant coffee powder, cocoa mix and cinnamon in blender container. Add almost boiling water. Blend on high speed until smooth. In a small saucepan, heat milk until steaming hot but not boiling. Pour into blender. Blend on high speed until foamy. Heat mugs by rinsing in hot water; dry thoroughly. Pour coffee mixture into heated mugs. Top with marshmallows and serve immediately. Makes 3 to 4 servings.

Whipping cream whips better if the bowl and beaters are chilled in the freezer before whipping the cream.

Iced Coffee Continental

Pour leftover breakfast coffee into ice cube trays and be ready for an afternoon treat.

2 to 3 cups prepared cold coffee
1/2 teaspoon Angostura bitters
1/2 teaspoon vanilla extract

2 tablespoons sugar
1-1/2 cups prepared hot or
    room temperature coffee

Pour the cold coffee into ice cube tray and freeze until firm. Stir bitters, vanilla extract and sugar into hot or room temperature coffee. Fill 2 tall glasses with frozen coffee cubes. Place a long teaspoon in each glass to prevent glass from cracking if hot coffee is added. Pour in hot or room temperature coffee and serve immediately. Makes 2 servings.

How To Make Iced Coffee Continental

1/Fill tall glasses with coffee ice cubes. If hot coffee is to be added to cold glass, stand a long spoon in the glass to prevent glass from cracking.

2/Pour mixture of bitters, vanilla sugar and coffee over ice cubes. Serve immediately.

Peachy Frosteds

Coffee and peaches blend in an exquisite summer cooler.

1 (16-oz.) can sliced peaches in syrup,
  undrained
1 cup cold milk

1 tablespoon instant coffee powder
1/2 pint vanilla ice cream
Maraschino cherries for garnish

Set aside 4 peach slices for garnish. Place remaining peaches in syrup, milk and instant coffee powder in blender container. Blend on high speed until smooth. Add ice cream. Blend until creamy. Pour into 4 glasses. Garnish with peach slices and maraschino cherries. Makes 4 servings.

Mocha Frosteds

Start this an hour or so before serving to give it time to cool.

1 cup prepared hot coffee
6 tablespoons chocolate syrup

1 pint vanilla ice cream, softened
1 cup prepared cold coffee

Place hot coffee and chocolate syrup in blender container. Blend until smooth. Cool to room temperature. Pour into a medium bowl. Add softened ice cream and cold coffee. With rotary beater, beat until smooth. Spoon into 4 tall glasses. Serve immediately. Makes 4 servings.

Cinnamon Cafe con Leche

Begin or end your day with this warming beverage.

2 teaspoons instant coffee powder
2 teaspoons sugar

2 cups very hot milk
2 cinnamon sticks, long enough to be stirrers

Place 1 teaspoon each instant coffee powder and sugar in 2 mugs. Pour in hot milk. Stir briskly with cinnamon stick. Leave in cinnamon sticks as stirrers. Serve immediately. Makes 2 servings.

For truly fresh-tasting iced coffee, pour freshly made hot coffee over a glass full of ice cubes. The fresher the coffee the fresher the taste.

Mint-Coffee Sodas

This one is for the young—in years or at heart.

3/4 cup hot water
4 teaspoons instant coffee powder
1/4 teaspoon peppermint extract,
    if desired

4 scoops peppermint ice cream
1-1/2 cups milk
About 1/2 (1-qt.) bottle club soda

Place hot water in a small pitcher. Stir in instant coffee powder until dissolved. Stir in peppermint extract, if desired. Pour equally into 4 ice cream soda glasses. Add 1 scoop ice cream to each glass. Pour milk equally into glasses and fill to brim with club soda. Serve with long-handled spoons and straws. Makes 4 servings.

Chocolate-Almond Sodas

Gather all the ice cream parlor chairs you can find and throw an ice cream soda party!

1 (3-oz.) Swiss bittersweet
    almond chocolate bar
2 tablespoons instant coffee powder
1/2 teaspoon almond extract

3/4 cup almost boiling water
1-1/2 cups milk
4 scoops coffee ice cream
About 1/2 (1-qt.) bottle club soda

Break chocolate bar into small pieces. Place in blender container. Add instant coffee powder, almond extract and almost boiling water. Blend on medium speed until smooth. Add milk. Blend. Place 1 scoop of ice cream in each of 4 ice cream soda glasses. Pour chocolate mixture equally into glasses. Fill with club soda. Serve with long-handled spoons and soda straws. Makes 4 servings.

Ice Cream Parlor Mocha Sodas

The best ice cream soda of all!

1/2 cup hot water
8 teaspoons instant coffee powder
2 cups milk
4 scoops chocolate ice cream

About 1/2 (1-qt.) bottle club soda
Sweetened Whipped Cream, page 122, or
    prepared whipped topping
Instant coffee powder for garnish

Place hot water in a medium pitcher. Stir in 8 teaspoons instant coffee powder until dissolved. Stir in milk. Place 1 scoop of ice cream in each of 4 ice cream soda glasses. Pour coffee-milk mixture equally into each glass. Fill glasses almost to brim with club soda. Top with Sweetened Whipped Cream or prepared whipped topping. If desired, sprinkle with instant coffee powder. Makes 4 servings.

Instant Mixes

Here are the instant coffee recipes you've been waiting for! So easy and quick, you can mix them up in just a few minutes. These are the delicious instant coffee mixes that warm you up on a cold afternoon, give you a brighter mid-morning pick-up or provide your guests with a sophisticated after-dinner coffee.

All you do is mix instant coffee with a few other ingredients. Mocha Mix is flavored with cocoa, vanilla and cinnamon. California Cappucino Mix uses orange extract, cinnamon and nutmeg.

All the mixes in this section can be blended in seconds and placed in airtight jars. I like to store mine in the refrigerator to ensure a fresh flavor. But these delicious mixes disappear long before they lose freshness. At coffee time, spoon the mix into a mug or pretty cup, add hot water and you have a coffee treat with a continental flair.

Coffee mixes make delightful gifts, too. You can give a large container of one kind of instant coffee mix or an assortment in several small containers. Be sure to include instructions on how much coffee mix to use for each cup of coffee.

Some other mixes to add to your shelf are the spiced sugar mixes at the end of this section. Just add a spoonful of one of these to a regular cup of coffee for a special lift. Viennese Sugar is flavored with almond and vanilla. Spiced Sugar adds a hint of cinnamon, nutmeg and cloves. And Espresso Sugar is a refreshing sweetener with grated lemon rind.

These mixes are wonderful to have on hand for impromptu guests. But why wait for company? When you want a cup of coffee with a little something extra, go to your mixes. Then relax and enjoy the delightful taste and aroma.

Dinner in Vienna

Veal Coffeenoff, page 37
Freshly Cooked Noodles
Tossed Green Salad
Crisp Apples & Camembert Cheese
Black Pepper Cookies, page 144
Viennese Coffee, page 20

Viennese Coffee Mix

From Vienna, where the coffee hour began.

1/4 cup sugar
1/4 teaspoon almond extract
1/4 teaspoon vanilla extract
3/4 cup instant coffee powder

1/2 cup nondairy creamer
1/2 cup instant nonfat dry milk powder
1 teaspoon cinnamon

Place sugar in a small bowl. Sprinkle with almond and vanilla extracts. With a fork, stir and blend until no trace of extract moisture remains. Add remaining ingredients. Stir. Sift to blend thoroughly. Store in an airtight container. To prepare 1 serving, spoon 2 to 3 teaspoons of mix into a standard size coffee cup. Fill to brim with almost boiling water; stir. Makes about 1-1/2 cups mix.

Café au Lait Mix

Try this for a special breakfast treat.

1/4 cup brown sugar, firmly packed
3/4 teaspoon vanilla extract
1/2 to 3/4 cup instant coffee powder

1/4 cup instant nonfat dry milk powder
1/4 cup nondairy creamer

Place sugar in a small bowl. Sprinkle with vanilla extract. With a fork, stir and blend until no trace of extract moisture remains. Add remaining ingredients. Stir. Sift to blend thoroughly. Store in an airtight container. To prepare 1 serving, spoon 2 to 3 teaspoons of mix into a standard size cup. Fill to brim with almost boiling water; stir. Makes 1-1/4 to 1-1/2 cups mix.

California Cappucino Mix

Reminds you of sunny California—or sunny Italy.

1/4 cup sugar
1 teaspoon orange extract
1/2 cup instant espresso coffee powder
1/4 cup instant nonfat dry milk powder

2 tablespoons nondairy creamer
1/8 teaspoon cinnamon
Dash nutmeg

Place sugar in a small bowl. Sprinkle with orange extract. With a fork, stir and blend until no trace of extract moisture remains. Add remaining ingredients. Stir. Sift to blend thoroughly. Store in an airtight container. To prepare 1 serving, spoon 2 to 3 teaspoons of mix into a standard size cup. Fill with almost boiling water; stir. Makes about 1 cup mix.

Mocha Mix

Even those few people who don't like coffee enjoy this—especially if it's topped with marshmallows!

1/2 cup sugar
1/2 teaspoon vanilla extract
1/2 cup instant coffee powder
1/4 cup cocoa powder

1/2 cup instant nonfat dry milk powder
2 tablespoons nondairy creamer
1/8 teaspoon cinnamon

Place sugar in a small bowl. Sprinkle with vanilla extract. With a fork, stir and blend until no trace of extract moisture remains. Add remaining ingredients. Stir. Sift to blend thoroughly. Store in an airtight container. To prepare 1 serving, spoon 2 to 3 teaspoons of mix into a standard size coffee cup; fill to brim with almost boiling water; stir. If desired, top with miniature marshmallows. Makes about 1-3/4 cups mix.

How To Make Mocha Mix

1/Sprinkle sugar with vanilla extract. With a fork blend vanilla into sugar. Stir in remaining ingredients and sift to blend thoroughly.

2/Store mix in an airtight container. To prepare 1 cup, pour hot water over 2 to 3 teaspoons of mix. Stir. Top with marshmallows, if desired.

Spiced Coffee Mix

Especially for those who take their coffee black.

1/4 cup sugar
1/2 teaspoon lemon extract
1/2 cup instant coffee powder
1/8 teaspoon cinnamon

Dash ground cloves
Dash ground allspice
Dash nutmeg

Place sugar in a small bowl. Sprinkle with lemon extract. With a fork, stir and blend until no trace of extract moisture remains. Add remaining ingredients. Stir. Sift to blend thoroughly. Store in an airtight container. To prepare 1 serving, spoon 2 to 3 teaspoons of mix into a standard size cup. Fill with almost boiling water; stir. Makes about 3/4 cup mix.

Turkish Coffee Mix

Let this exotic blend take you away from it all.

1/4 cup light brown sugar, firmly packed
1 teaspoon orange extract
1/2 cup instant coffee powder

1/4 teaspoon ground ginger
1/8 teaspoon ground cloves

Place sugar in a small bowl. Sprinkle with orange extract. With a fork, stir and blend until no trace of extract moisture remains. Add remaining ingredients. Stir. Sift to blend thoroughly. Store in an airtight container. To prepare 1 serving, spoon 2 to 3 teaspoons of mix into a standard size cup. Fill with almost boiling water; stir. Makes about 3/4 cup mix.

Spiced Low-Calorie Coffee Mix

Who says dieters have to go without?

6 tablespoons instant coffee powder
4 tablespoons instant nonfat dry milk powder
2 tablespoons granulated sugar substitute
1/8 teaspoon cinnamon

1/8 teaspoon nutmeg
1/8 teaspoon ground ginger
1/2 teaspoon vanilla extract

In a small bowl, combine all ingredients except vanilla extract. Stir to blend. Sprinkle with vanilla extract. With a fork or wooden spoon, stir and press until no trace of extract moisture remains. Sift to blend thoroughly. Store in an airtight container. To prepare 1 serving, spoon 2 to 3 teaspoons of mix into a standard size cup. Fill with almost boiling water; stir. Makes about 3/4 cup mix.

Viennese Sugar

A spoonful of this adds more than sugar to your cup!

1 cup sugar
3/4 teaspoon vanilla extract

1/4 teaspoon almond extract

Place sugar in a small bowl. Sprinkle with vanilla and almond extracts. With a fork, stir to blend well. Store in an airtight container. Use to sweeten coffee to taste. Makes about 1 cup flavored sugar.

Espresso Sugar

If you can't afford a Roman holiday, try this.

1 cup sugar
1 teaspoon grated lemon rind

Place sugar in a small bowl. Sprinkle with grated lemon rind. Stir to mix well. Store in an airtight container in the refrigerator. Use to sweeten black coffee to taste. Makes about 1 cup flavored sugar.

Spiced Sugar

You're sure to find other uses for this scrumptious sugar.

1 cup sugar
1/2 teaspoon cinnamon

1/8 teaspoon nutmeg
1/8 teaspoon ground cloves

Place sugar in a small bowl. Sprinkle with spices. Stir to mix well. Store in an airtight container. Use to sweeten coffee to taste. Makes about 1 cup flavored sugar.

Extract flavors evaporate quickly when left uncovered, so keep the bottle closed except to pour out the amount you need.

Main Dishes

The task of combining taste appeal, good nutrition and ease of preparation, while keeping a close eye on your pocketbook isn't easy. Add to this the desire for new and different experiences and the job seems insurmountable. It's easy to come up with creative meals if you're not concerned about money or time. It's another thing to make exciting meals from everyday fare. Even filet mignon served night after night loses its appeal and might as well be cornmeal mush.

Help is at hand with coffee. Yes, coffee! It can add rich taste and new flavor! For example, Meatballs Smitaine are small, well-flavored meatballs in a tangy sauce laced with coffee. Add fluffy rice and freshly cooked green beans for a meal both different and delicious. Try coffee-spiced Meat Loaf Ring for a new great taste. Fill the center with creamy mashed potatoes and vegetables. Then there is Quick Boston Baked Beans cooked in a coffee-molasses sauce. They need only a big bowl of coleslaw and perhaps Glazed Apple Pie, page 112, for a super Saturday night supper. Humble vegetables like Carrots & Potatoes in Coffee Cream are a gourmet experience. Or try Creamy Potatoes with glazed ham steak for Sunday brunch.

You may cast a doubting eye on a recipe calling for coffee with meat or beans or barbecue sauce, but the truth is that coffee, like wine, is not obvious in the completed dish. For example, when you add wine to a beef stew or casserole, you pour in the specified amount without a second thought. When the final dish is served you cannot detect a pronounced flavor of the wine itself but there is a richness and depth of flavor that would be missing if the wine were omitted. So in the following recipes you won't taste the coffee, but you will notice the new character and rich flavor coffee adds.

A Festive
Sunday Brunch

Icy Cold Compote of Apple Slices
Halved Green Grapes,
Orange & Grapefruit Sections
Flaming Highland Ham, page 33
Creamy Potatoes, page 34
Swedish Christmas Coffeecake, page 42
Hot Coffee

Western-Style Hamburgers

The zesty coffee-chili sauce makes the difference.

2 tablespoons vegetable oil
1 large purple onion, peeled and
   finely minced
2 garlic cloves, peeled and
   finely minced
1 cup chili sauce
1 tablespoon jalapeño relish

1/2 cup prepared coffee
1 tablespoon more vegetable oil
1-1/2 lbs. lean ground beef
3 hamburger buns, halved
   and toasted
1 cup grated sharp Cheddar cheese

Heat 2 tablespoons oil in a medium skillet. Sauté onion and garlic in oil over low heat until soft but not brown. Add chili sauce and jalapeño relish. Bring to a boil. Lower heat and simmer 5 minutes. Stir in coffee. Keep on low heat 5 to 10 minutes but do not boil after adding coffee. Remove from heat. Keep warm. Heat 1 tablespoon oil in a large skillet. Shape meat into 6 thick patties. Brown in oil over high heat. Turn patties; lower heat. Cook 5 to 10 minutes. Place on toasted buns. Cover with hot sauce and top with grated cheese. Serve immediately. Makes 6 servings.

Meatballs Smitaine

Coffee enriches the natural flavors.

2 tablespoons butter or margarine
1 medium onion, finely chopped
1 small garlic clove, peeled and minced
1-1/2 lbs. lean ground beef
1 teaspoon imported paprika
1 teaspoon salt
1 cup soft breadcrumbs
2 teaspoons Worcestershire sauce
1 egg

1/2 cup flour
1/3 lb. salt pork
1 cup prepared coffee
1/2 cup dry red wine
1/2 cup beef broth or water
1 cup dairy sour cream, room temperature
Salt to taste
4 cups hot cooked flat noodles or rice
Paprika for garnish

Melt butter or margarine in a small skillet. Sauté onion and garlic until limp. Place meat in a large bowl. Scrape contents of skillet over meat. Add 1 teaspoon paprika, 1 teaspoon salt, breadcrumbs, Worcestershire sauce and egg. Mix thoroughly. Form into 1-inch meatballs. Roll in flour. Set aside. Rinse excess salt from salt pork. Blot dry with paper towels. Cut into small dice. Cook in a large skillet over low heat until fat is rendered and dice are crisp. Remove dice; drain on paper towels. Heat rendered fat in skillet. Shake excess flour from meatballs. Sauté a few at a time until lightly browned. Pour drippings from skillet and discard. Return meatballs to skillet. Add coffee, wine and broth or water. Simmer over low heat 30 minutes. Gently stir in sour cream and salt pork dice. Stir until heated. Add salt to taste. Spoon over hot flat noodles or rice. Sprinkle with paprika. Makes 6 to 8 servings.

Meat Loaf Ring

Pile creamy potatoes and vegetables in the center of the ring.

1-1/2 lbs. lean ground beef
1 lb. lean ground veal
1/2 lb. lean ground pork
1-1/2 cups soft breadcrumbs
3/4 cup prepared coffee
1 egg, slightly beaten
1 tablespoon prepared mustard
1 tablespoon Worcestershire sauce
1 teaspoon salt
6 medium white potatoes

Water
3 tablespoons butter or margarine
1/4 cup minced onion
1 tablespoon more butter or margarine
2 (10-oz.) pkgs. frozen mixed vegetables,
   partly thawed
4 tablespoons more water
2 tablespoons more prepared coffee
1 tablespoon minced parsley

Preheat oven to 350°F (175°C). Lightly oil a 10-inch ring mold. Combine beef, veal, pork, breadcrumbs, 3/4 cup coffee, egg, mustard, Worcestershire sauce and salt. Blend well. Pack lightly into prepared mold. Bake in preheated oven 45 to 50 minutes. While meat loaf bakes, boil potatoes in water to cover until tender. Peel while hot and mash with 3 tablespoons butter or margarine until smooth. Keep warm. In a medium saucepan, sauté onion in 1 tablespoon butter or margarine until limp. Add frozen vegetables, 4 tablespoons water and 2 tablespoons coffee. Bring to a boil. Cover and lower heat. Cook until tender. Drain; add hot cooking liquid to mashed potatoes. Beat until blended. Fold cooked vegetables and minced parsley into mashed potatoes. To serve, unmold meat loaf onto round serving platter. Fill center of ring with potatoes and vegetables. Serve remaining vegetables separately. Makes 6 to 8 servings.

Jamaican Stuffed Peppers

Try a little magic from the Caribbean.

6 large green peppers
Water
4 tablespoons butter or margarine
1 large purple onion, peeled and minced
1/2 lb. lean ground pork
1/2 lb. lean ground beef
1/2 teaspoon salt

1/2 teaspoon black pepper
1/2 cup seedless raisins
2 cups cooked rice
1 cup prepared coffee
1 egg, well beaten
1/4 cup pignoli nuts, if desired
3 tablespoons fine dry breadcrumbs

In a large saucepan, boil whole peppers in water to cover 2 or 3 minutes. Dry carefully to remove wax coating. Cut off stem end; scoop out white membrane and seeds. Melt butter or margarine in a large skillet. Sauté onion until limp. Add pork and beef. Cook until lightly browned. Add remaining ingredients except breadcrumbs. Cook over medium heat 6 to 8 minutes until blended or until liquid is absorbed. Preheat oven to 350°F (175°C). Stuff peppers with meat mixture. Sprinkle lightly with breadcrumbs. Place in a baking pan and cover with aluminum foil. Bake in preheated oven 15 minutes. Remove foil and bake 15 to 20 minutes. Makes 6 servings.

Easy Empanadas

One of South America's favorite appetizers can double as a main course.

2 tablespoons butter or margarine
2 purple onions, peeled and finely minced
2 garlic cloves, peeled and finely minced
1 green pepper, seeded and finely minced
2 to 4 canned whole jalapeño peppers,
   seeded, drained and minced
1/2 cup chopped black olives

1 cup prepared coffee
1-1/2 lbs. lean ground beef
1/2 teaspoon salt
1 teaspoon black pepper
9 frozen patty shells (1-1/2 pkgs.),
   partly thawed

Melt butter or margarine in a large skillet. Sauté onions, garlic and green pepper over very low heat until limp but not brown. Add jalapeño peppers, olives and coffee. Cook over low heat until ingredients are soft and mixture is blended. Add beef, breaking up with a fork. Simmer, stirring occasionally, until lightly browned. Add salt and pepper. Cook over low heat until most of liquid has evaporated. Preheat oven to 400°F (205°C). On a lightly floured surface, roll out a patty shell to a 6-1/2 to 7-inch circle. Cut in half. Spoon about 2 tablespoons meat mixture on one side of each half circle. Fold over and seal edges with fork tines. Repeat with remaining patty shells and meat mixture. Place on ungreased baking sheets. Bake in preheated oven 10 minutes; lower heat to 300°F (150°C) and bake 15 more minutes. Serve hot. Makes 18 empanadas.

Barbecued Spareribs

Especially good with baked sweet potatoes and crisp coleslaw.

5 to 6 lbs. spareribs, cut in
   serving-size pieces
Water
1 cup prepared coffee
1 cup molasses

1/2 teaspoon salt
1/3 cup prepared mustard
1 tablespoon Worcestershire sauce
1/2 cup cider vinegar
2 to 3 dashes hot red pepper sauce

Preheat oven to 350°F (175°C). Arrange spareribs 1 layer deep on a rack in a large, shallow roasting pan. Add water to cover bottom of pan. Roast 1 hour in preheated oven. Pour drippings from pan. Remove rack and place ribs in pan. In a small saucepan, combine remaining ingredients. Stir over medium heat until blended and steaming. Pour over ribs. Bake 1/2 hour, basting frequently with sauce. Makes 8 servings.

Make sure the ground beef you buy is lean. Otherwise you are pouring money down the drain with excess grease and decreasing the amount of meat protein in the meal.

Coffee-Glazed Duck

Crisp browned duck makes a festive entree.

1 (3- to 4-lb.) duck, thawed but cold
1 large onion, peeled and studded with cloves
1 large crisp apple, halved
2 or 3 celery stalks

1 bay leaf
1 teaspoon salt
Water
Coffee Glaze, see below

Coffee Glaze:
1 (8-oz.) jar honey (1 cup)
4 tablespoons frozen orange juice concentrate

2 teaspoons cornstarch
2 tablespoons instant coffee powder

Cut off excess fat at tail end of duck. Prick duck in several places with the tip of a sharp knife. Place with onion, apple, celery, bay leaf and salt in a large pot. Cover with water. Bring to a boil. Skim until clear. Lower heat and simmer 1-1/2 to 2 hours or until duck is very tender. Remove duck from broth and cool. Prepare Coffee Glaze. Cut duck into quarters. With fingers carefully pull out and discard leg bones, back bone and rib cage. Place duck on broiler rack. Brush both sides with glaze; let stand 20 to 30 minutes. Preheat broiler. Turn duck skin-side up and brush again with glaze. Broil 10 to 15 minutes, turning occasionally and basting frequently with glaze. Makes 4 generous servings.

Coffee Glaze:
In a small saucepan, combine honey and frozen orange juice concentrate. Bring to a full boil. Remove from heat. Dissolve cornstarch in about 1 tablespoon of honey mixture. Add to remaining honey mixture. Place on low heat. Stir in instant coffee powder. Cook only until slightly thickened, smooth and blended. Makes about 1 cup.

Country Ham With Red-Eye Gravy

Treat yourself to a Southern favorite.

4 (1/2-inch thick) slices country-cured ham
Cold water

3/4 cup boiling water
2 tablespoons prepared coffee

Place ham in a large shallow baking pan. Cover with cold water. Let stand 6 to 8 hours. Drain and blot dry with paper towels. Remove and discard rind. In an ungreased large skillet over medium-high heat, fry ham slices 5 to 6 minutes on each side. Place on a warm serving platter. Pour off all but 2 tablespoons drippings from skillet. Add boiling water and continue to boil, scraping skillet with spatula to pick up all flavorful bits of ham. Stir in coffee. Blend well. Pour over ham slices. Serve immediately. Makes 4 servings.

Chicken Montego

Easy patty shells full of tender chicken in an exotic cream sauce.

8 frozen patty shells (1 pkg. plus 2)
1 (10-1/2-oz.) can chicken broth
1/2 can water
2 chicken breasts, cut in half
4 tablespoons butter or margarine
4 tablespoons flour

1 cup prepared coffee
1/2 cup dairy sour cream, room temperature
2 tablespoons minced black olives
1 (2-oz.) jar chopped pimientos
1/2 cup slivered Brazil nuts

Bake patty shells according to package directions. Combine chicken broth and water in a large saucepan. Bring to a boil. Add chicken breasts. Lower heat and simmer about 15 minutes until chicken is tender. Cool. Melt butter or margarine in a deep skillet. Stir in flour. Cook over low heat 2 to 3 minutes. Slowly add 1-1/2 cups cooled chicken broth. Stir over low heat until very thick and smooth. Slowly add coffee, blending well. Stir in sour cream, olives, pimientos and Brazil nuts. Cook over low heat until sauce is thickened and blended. Remove from heat. Remove skin and bones from chicken breasts. Cut chicken into bite-size pieces. Add to sauce. Heat to steaming. Serve over patty shells. Makes 8 servings.

Sliced Beef With Brown Gravy

A superb dinner for family or guests.

1/4 lb. beef suet
1/4 cup flour
1/2 teaspoon salt
1 teaspoon pepper
1 (4 to 4-1/2-lb.) pot roast, room temperature
1 large onion, peeled and quartered
1 large carrot, cut in 1-inch pieces

1 medium tomato, quartered
1 stalk celery, with leaves, cut in 1-inch pieces
1 garlic clove, peeled
1 cup prepared coffee
1-1/2 cups beef broth
1-1/2 cups water

Dice beef suet and cook in a Dutch oven or heavy pot over low heat until fat is rendered. With slotted spoon remove and discard suet. Combine flour, salt and pepper in a large shallow bowl. Blot beef completely dry with paper towels. Dredge in flour mixture. Press flour into meat; shake off excess. Reserve remaining flour for gravy. Heat rendered fat in pot. Add meat and brown well on all sides. Remove pot from heat and spoon off as much fat as possible. Return to heat and add all remaining ingredients. Bring to a full boil. Lower heat and simmer partly covered 2-1/2 to 3 hours or until tender; turn meat several times. Remove meat from pot. Cool liquid slightly; strain into a second large pot or bowl. Discard vegetables. Add meat to liquid. Cool. Refrigerate several hours or overnight until all fat is congealed on the surface. Remove congealed fat. Remove meat from liquid and slice. Heat liquid. Stir a little of the liquid into the reserved seasoned flour. Stir flour-liquid mixture into remaining liquid. Stir until slightly thickened. Add meat slices and heat to serving temperature. To serve, arrange meat slices on a long platter; spoon gravy over meat slices. Serve remaining gravy separately. Makes about 8 servings.

Coffee-Glazed Baked Ham

Leftover ham makes marvelous casseroles. Try Casserole au Gratin, page 36.

1 (1-lb.) can apricot halves in heavy syrup
1 cup honey
4 tablespoons instant coffee powder
1 teaspoon cinnamon
1/4 teaspoon ground cloves

1 (6- to 8-lb.) uncooked half ham
Whole cloves
Water
Parsley sprigs for garnish

Preheat oven to 350°F (175°C). Drain syrup from apricot halves into a small saucepan; reserve apricot halves. Add honey, instant coffee powder, cinnamon and ground cloves to syrup. Stir over low heat until coffee dissolves. Simmer glaze over very low heat 15 minutes, stirring occasionally. Remove from heat and cool at room temperature. Place ham on a rack in a shallow roasting pan. Bake in preheated oven 2-1/2 to 3-1/2 hours or 25 minutes per pound. One hour before baking time is completed, remove ham from oven. Remove rind and all but about 1/2 inch of fat. Score remaining fat diagonally in both directions to make a diamond pattern. Place a whole clove in center of each diamond. Pour water into roasting pan to cover bottom of pan. Baste ham with glaze; reserve remaining glaze. Return ham to oven. Bake 45 minutes, basting with some of the glaze every 15 minutes. Place apricot halves on rack around ham. Baste ham and apricots with glaze. Bake for a final 15 minutes. Remove from oven and baste ham several times with remaining glaze. Place on serving platter and surround with apricot halves. Garnish with parsley sprigs. Makes 12 to 16 servings.

Quick Boston Baked Beans

Authentic homecooked flavor in a fraction of the time.

1/4 lb. salt pork
1 medium onion, peeled and chopped
2 (1-lb.) cans Boston-style baked beans
1/2 cup molasses

1/2 cup prepared coffee
1/2 teaspoon dry mustard
1/2 teaspoon pepper

Rinse loose salt from salt pork under cold running water. Blot dry with paper towel. Cut into 1/4-inch dice. Place in a large skillet over low heat. Cook, stirring frequently, until crisp. Remove from skillet and set aside. Sauté chopped onion in drippings over medium heat until soft. Preheat oven to 350°F (175°C). Place beans in a deep casserole or bean pot. Stir in sautéed onion and crisp pork dice. In a small bowl, combine molasses, coffee, mustard and pepper. Pour over beans. Bake uncovered in preheated oven 45 minutes to 1 hour until liquid is nearly absorbed and top is crisp. Makes 6 to 8 servings.

Carrots & Potatoes in Coffee Cream

Perfect with broiled meat or fish.

2 cups thinly sliced carrots
1/2 teaspoon salt
Water
6 very small new potatoes,
   unpeeled and boiled

1 cup dairy sour cream,
   room temperature
1/2 cup coffee
1 teaspoon paprika

Place carrots and salt in a large saucepan with enough water to cover. Boil uncovered until tender and almost dry. Drain and keep hot. Cut boiled potatoes in quarters. Add to carrots. Mix sour cream and coffee together. Add to vegetables. Heat until steaming; do not boil after adding sour cream. Sprinkle with paprika and serve at once. Makes 6 servings.

Flaming Highland Ham

A colorful and dramatic performance!

1 (1-inch thick) fully cooked ham steak
2 tablespoons light brown sugar
2 tablespoons mustard

1/8 teaspoon ginger
6 tablespoons brandy
2 tablespoons prepared hot coffee

Preheat broiler. Slash edges of ham steak through fat to prevent curling. In a small bowl, combine brown sugar, mustard and ginger. Stir in 2 tablespoons brandy to form a paste. Place remaining brandy in a small pitcher in a pan of hot water to keep warm. Spread steak with half of sugar paste. Broil about 4 inches from high heat 5 to 6 minutes. Turn; spread with remaining sugar paste. Broil until surface is glazed. Place steak on a warm heat resistant platter. Bring platter to the table. Pour warm brandy over and ignite. Let flame briefly. Pour coffee over flames to extinguish. Slice and serve, spooning some of the brandy-coffee sauce over each portion. Makes 3 to 4 servings.

Chili powder tends to lose its flavor as it sits on the shelf. To ensure fresh flavor, if you can't remember when you bought your chili powder, replace it with new.

Creamy Potatoes

Add grilled sausage and apple rings for a special Sunday morning brunch.

2 tablespoons butter or margarine
2 medium, purple onions,
   peeled and finely chopped
4 medium potatoes, boiled,
   peeled and cubed

1 (2-oz.) jar chopped pimientos
1 teaspoon salt
1 teaspoon pepper
4 tablespoons light cream
1 cup prepared coffee

Melt butter or margarine in a large skillet. Sauté onions over low heat until soft. Add remaining ingredients. Mix well. Cook uncovered over very low heat until liquid has evaporated and potatoes are creamy. Serve hot. Makes 4 to 6 servings.

Breakfast Corned Beef Hash

Change your Sunday morning breakfast habit with this fabulous hash platter!

2 tablespoons butter or margarine
1 tablespoon vegetable oil
1 medium, mild purple onion,
   peeled and chopped
1 medium, green pepper, seeded and chopped
2 (1-lb.) cans corned beef hash
1/2 cup prepared coffee
Broiled Apricots, see below

1 teaspoon Worcestershire sauce
1 teaspoon Dijon or similar hot mustard
4 tablespoons dairy sour cream,
   room temperature
Salt to taste
Coarse ground black pepper to taste
1/4 cup minced parsley

Broiled Apricots:

1 (1-lb.) can apricot halves
2 tablespoons brown sugar

2 tablespoons butter or margarine,
   cut in slivers

Melt butter or margarine in oil in a large skillet. Sauté onion and green pepper over low heat until soft. Add corned beef hash. Break up hash with a wooden spoon. Add coffee. Simmer over medium heat until coffee is absorbed. Remove from heat. Prepare Broiled Apricots. Stir Worcestershire sauce, mustard and sour cream into hash. Stir over low heat until very hot; do not boil after adding sour cream. Season with salt and pepper to taste. Spoon onto serving platter. Sprinkle with minced parsley and surround with Broiled Apricots. Makes 6 to 8 servings.

Broiled Apricots:
Preheat oven to 350°F (175°C). Place in a shallow baking pan. Sprinkle each half with brown sugar and dot with butter or margarine slivers. Place in preheated oven 10 minutes then under high broiler heat until glazed.

California Chili

Serve tortilla chips with this easy-to-prepare one-dish meal.

1 medium, purple onion, peeled and minced	1 large tomato
1 tablespoon vegetable oil	1 large avocado
1 tablespoon chili powder	1/4 cup minced green onion
2 (1-lb.) cans chili with meat and beans	1/4 cup minced parsley
1/2 cup prepared coffee	1/2 cup grated Cheddar cheese
2 tablespoons canned jalapeño sauce, if desired	

In a large saucepan, sauté onion in oil over low heat until very soft. Stir in chili powder. Add canned chili, coffee and, if desired, jalapeño sauce. Bring to a boil, stirring constantly. Lower heat and simmer very slowly about 5 minutes. Cut tomato into 8 wedges. Gently squeeze out seeds. Cut avocado in half and remove seed. Cut avocado into 8 wedges and remove peel. Spoon hot chili into 4 bowls. Top each with 2 tomato wedges and 2 avocado wedges. Sprinkle with minced green onion, parsley and grated cheese. Makes 4 servings.

How To Make California Chili

1/Simmer together sautéed onion, chili powder, canned chili, coffee and jalapeño sauce.

2/Spoon chili into individual bowls. Place tomato and avocado wedges on top of each serving. Garnish with minced onion, parsley and grated Cheddar cheese.

Casserole au Gratin

Ham, artichokes and green beans make an easy and delicious one-dish meal.

1/2 cup water
1 (10-oz.) pkg. frozen cut green beans
1 (10-oz.) pkg. frozen artichokes au gratin,
   thawed
1-1/2 cups diced cooked ham
3 tablespoons butter or margarine

3 tablespoons flour
1 cup prepared cold coffee
4 tablespoons grated cheese
2 tablespoons mayonnaise
1 cup fine dry breadcrumbs
Paprika for garnish

Preheat oven to 350°F (175°C). Bring water to a boil. Add green beans. Cook until just tender. Drain and place in the bottom of a 1-quart casserole. Remove artichoke hearts from sauce; reserve sauce. Cut artichokes into bite-size pieces. Place with ham on top of green beans. Melt butter or margarine in a small saucepan. Stir in flour. Stir over very low heat 2 or 3 minutes. Slowly stir in coffee. Continue to stir over low heat until sauce begins to thicken. Remove from heat. Add grated cheese, mayonnaise and reserved artichoke sauce. Stir until cheese melts and sauce is smooth. Pour over ham and vegetables in casserole. Cover evenly with breadcrumbs. Sprinkle lightly with paprika. Bake in preheated oven 25 to 30 minutes. Makes 6 to 8 servings.

Better Beef Stew

Tender slices of lean beef in a rich sauce with vegetables.

1/4 lb. salt pork
1-1/2 lbs. lean top round of beef,
   sliced 1/8 inch thick
2-1/2 cups sliced carrots
12 very small white onions, peeled
1 tablespoon butter or margarine,
   cut in slivers

1 (10-1/2-oz.) can beef broth
1 (8-oz.) can tomato sauce
1/2 cup prepared coffee
1/4 teaspoon Worcestershire sauce
1 teaspoon Dijon or similar hot mustard
Salt and pepper to taste
1 cup cooked green peas

Wash excess salt from salt pork. Blot dry and dice. Cook in a large heavy skillet over low heat until fat is rendered and dice are crisp. Remove dice; drain on paper towels. Pour off and reserve all but a thin layer of fat from skillet. Turn heat on high. Quickly brown beef slices on both sides 2 or 3 slices at a time, adding additional rendered fat as needed. Place in a long shallow baking dish. Top with sliced carrots and onions. Add butter or margarine slivers. Preheat oven to 375°F (190°C). Pour broth, tomato sauce and coffee into same skillet used to brown beef slices. Add Worcestershire sauce and mustard. Mix well. Bring to a boil, lower heat and simmer 5 minutes. Add salt and pepper to taste. Pour over meat and vegetables. Cover baking pan with aluminum foil and seal. Bake in preheated oven 2 hours or until meat is tender. Stir in peas. Makes 6 servings.

Veal Coffeenoff

Stroganoff with a Brazilian flavor.

2 tablespoons butter or margarine
1 garlic clove, peeled and minced
1 large onion, peeled and chopped
1/2 cup flour
1/4 teaspoon pepper
1/2 teaspoon salt
1-1/2 lbs. lean veal,
    cut across grain in thin strips
2 tablespoons more butter or margarine

1 tablespoon Worcestershire sauce
1 cup chicken broth
1-1/2 cups prepared coffee
1/4 cup chopped fresh parsley
1 (8-oz.) carton dairy sour cream,
    room temperature
1/4 cup more flour
1 (8-oz.) pkg. flat noodles,
    cooked according to pkg. directions

In a 2-quart Dutch oven or heavy pot over medium heat, melt 2 tablespoons butter or margarine. Add garlic and onion. Sauté until soft but not browned. Remove from pot and set aside. In a shallow bowl, combine 1/2 cup flour, pepper and salt. Dredge veal strips in flour mixture. Melt 2 tablespoons butter or margarine in pot. Brown veal strips. Add onion and garlic, Worcestershire sauce, chicken broth and coffee. Bring to a boil over medium heat. Lower heat. Cover and simmer 1-1/2 hours or until veal is very tender. Stir in parsley. Lower heat to stop boiling. In a small bowl, blend sour cream and 1/4 cup flour. Add to hot liquid. Cook and stir until thick and creamy but do not boil after adding sour cream. Serve over hot cooked noodles. Makes 4 to 6 servings.

Sour cream will not curdle when added to a hot sauce if the sauce is not boiling and the sour cream is at room temperature. Stir the sour cream into the sauce very slowly. Heat through but do not boil after sour cream has been added.

Breads

In medieval times a baker of inferior bread could be publicly whipped. When you taste the spongy soggy mass that sometimes passes for bread you may long for such customs to return.

There is nothing like homemade bread and it's actually easy and fun to make. In fact, if you are mad at the world, a good workout kneading bread can calm your nerves and soothe your troubled spirit. If, on the other hand, all is well, you'll find joy in making bread and filling your kitchen with its heavenly fragrance.

Why not make your bread baking extra special? Give each one a new flavor difference, a new taste appeal, with coffee. Coffee can turn an ordinary whole-wheat loaf into a bread so delicious it needs only butter for a super treat. Don't take my word for it. Try Country-Style Whole-Wheat Bread yourself. Then there is Sicilian Bread, a loaf inspired by the crusty breads of Sicily. It's an unsurpassed compliment to an antipasto platter. And don't wait for Christmas to serve fruit-filled Swedish Christmas Coffeecake. Your next Sunday brunch will do.

Yeast breads do require careful attention to the temperature guides given in each recipe, but yeast is not as tempermental as many people believe. As for rising in a warm draft-free spot, I find the easiest way to solve this problem is to place the dough in the oven. First heat the oven to 200°F (95°C). Turn off the heat and let the oven cool with the door open 10 to 15 minutes. Then place the dough in the still warm oven and close the door. It will rise perfectly.

Coffee adds special flavor to quick breads too. I have included muffins, a steamed bread and even Great Griddle Cakes to be devoured with Maple-Coffee Syrup.

Saturday Night Supper
Quick Boston Baked Beans, page 32
Coffee-Can Date-Nut Bread, page 48
Coleslaw
Glazed Apple Pie, page 112
Hot Coffee

Country-Style Whole-Wheat Bread

Packed with homemade country-kitchen flavor.

3 tablespoons instant coffee powder
1/4 cup hot water
1/2 cup warm water (110°F, 45°C)
1 tablespoon sugar
2 envelopes active dry yeast
3 cups unbleached white flour

1 cup stone-ground whole-wheat flour
1/4 cup more sugar
1 teaspoon salt
1 cup milk
1/3 to 1 cup more unbleached white flour
1 tablespoon stone-ground yellow cornmeal

Dissolve instant coffee powder in hot water; set aside and cool to lukewarm. Pour warm water into a large bowl. Add sugar and yeast. Let stand about 10 minutes or until yeast dissolves and mixture is very bubbly. Add 3 cups unbleached white flour, whole-wheat flour, sugar, salt, dissolved instant coffee and milk. Beat until blended. Add enough unbleached white flour, 1/3 cup at a time, to make a soft dough. On a lightly floured surface, knead 5 minutes or until dough forms a smooth satiny ball. Generously butter a large bowl. Place dough in bowl. Turn dough to coat with butter. Cover and let rise in a warm place until doubled in bulk, about 1-1/2 hours. Generously butter a 9" x 5" loaf pan. Punch down dough. On a very lightly floured surface, shape into a loaf to fit into prepared pan. Sprinkle top of loaf with cornmeal. Let rise in a warm place until doubled in bulk, about 1 hour. Preheat oven to 375°F (190°C). Bake loaf in preheated oven about 1 hour or until golden. If loaf browns too quickly, cover loosely with aluminum foil. Loaf is done if it sounds hollow when tapped. Turn out on a rack and cool completely before serving. Makes one 9-inch loaf.

New England Oatmeal Bread

The recipe makes 2 loaves; give one to a friend.

1 cup quick cooking oatmeal
1 cup prepared hot coffee
2 tablespoons butter or margarine,
    room temperature
4 tablespoons dark brown sugar

1 teaspoon salt
1 envelope active dry yeast
1/2 cup prepared warm coffee
    (110°F, 45°C)
3-1/2 to 4 cups all-purpose flour

Place oatmeal in a large bowl. Add hot coffee, butter or margarine, brown sugar and salt. Stir until butter melts and sugar and salt dissolve. Cool to room temperature. Sprinkle yeast over 1/2 cup warm coffee. Let stand about 10 minutes or until yeast dissolves and mixture is bubbly. Stir into oatmeal mixture. Add 3 cups flour. Stir until blended. Cover and let rise in a warm place until doubled in bulk. Coat two 9" x 5" loaf pans with vegetable shortening; set aside. Punch down dough. On a lightly floured surface, knead 2 to 3 minutes, adding more flour if dough is too soft to form into loaves. Divide dough in half; form into 2 loaves. Place in prepared pans. Cover and let rise until doubled in bulk. Preheat oven to 375°F (190°C). Bake loaves 40 to 50 minutes until well browned. If loaves brown too quickly, cover loosely with aluminum foil. Loaves are done if they sound hollow when tapped. Makes 2 loaves.

Sicilian Bread

So good with meatballs and spaghetti in a rich tomato sauce.

2 tablespoons vegetable shortening	1 tablespoon sugar
1 tablespoon butter or margarine, room temperature	1 cup warm water (110°F, 45°C)
1 cup prepared coffee	2 cups all-purpose flour
1 tablespoon molasses	1-3/4 cups cracked wheat
2 teaspoons salt	2 cups more all-purpose flour
2 envelopes active dry yeast	About 1/4 cup cornmeal
	About 2 teaspoons milk

In a small saucepan, combine shortening, butter or margarine, coffee, molasses and salt. Stir over low heat until butter or margarine and shortening melt and mixture is smooth. Cool to lukewarm, 110° to 115°F (45°C). Put yeast and sugar in a large bowl. Add warm water. Let stand about 10 minutes or until yeast dissolves and mixture is bubbly. Add coffee mixture and 2 cups flour. Beat with electric mixer on low speed 30 seconds. Stir in cracked wheat with a wooden spoon until blended. Stir in 2 cups flour. Cover and let rise in a warm place until doubled in bulk. On a lightly floured surface, knead dough for a minute. Divide in half. Shape each half into a ball. Cover and let rise until doubled in bulk. Cover a baking sheet with cornmeal; set aside. On a lightly floured surface knead each ball about 1 minute; shape each into a long, narrow loaf. Place on prepared baking sheet. With a sharp knife make 3 or 4 diagonal cuts about 1/4 inch deep across tops of loaves. Cover and let rise until doubled in bulk. Preheat oven to 375°F (190°C). Place a shallow pan of water on bottom rack to help crusts harden. Brush tops of loaves with milk to help brown. Bake in preheated oven 35 to 40 minutes. If loaves brown too quickly, cover loosely with aluminum foil. Makes 2 loaves.

Temperature of the ingredients is important in bread making. Too much heat kills the live yeast and not enough heat slows down its action. Dissolve active dry yeast in warm water, 110°F to 115°F (45°C). A few drops on the inside of your wrist should feel slightly warm.

Double-Coffee Coffeecake

Cups of steaming coffee or hot chocolate make this an extra-special treat.

1 envelope active dry yeast
1/2 cup warm water (110°F, 45°C)
2 tablespoons brown sugar
1/2 cup prepared coffee
2 tablespoons butter or margarine,
   room temperature

1 egg
1-1/2 cups all-purpose flour
1 teaspoon salt
2 to 2-1/2 cups more all-purpose flour
Coffee-Sugar Filling, see below
Brown Sugar Glaze, see below

Coffee-Sugar Filling:
3 tablespoons brown sugar
4 tablespoons butter or margarine,
   room temperature
2 teaspoons instant coffee powder

1/2 teaspoon cinnamon
1/4 teaspoon nutmeg
1/4 teaspoon ground allspice

Brown Sugar Glaze:
5 tablespoons brown sugar
3 tablespoons butter or margarine,
   room temperature

Sprinkle yeast over warm water in a large bowl. Stir in 1 teaspoon brown sugar. Let stand until bubbly. In a small saucepan, combine remaining brown sugar, coffee and butter or margarine. Stir over low heat until butter or margarine melts. Cool slightly. Add to yeast mixture. Add egg; beat with electric mixer on medium speed until blended. Add 1-1/2 cups flour and the salt. Beat with electric mixer on low speed about 1 minute. Add 2 cups flour. Beat with a wooden spoon about 2 minutes until blended and smooth. Stir in more flour if needed to make a soft dough. On a lightly floured surface, knead until dough forms a smooth satiny ball. Generously butter a large bowl. Place dough in bowl; turn to coat with butter. Cover and let rise in a warm place until doubled in bulk. Prepare Coffee-Sugar Filling; set aside. Punch down dough. On a lightly floured surface, divide dough in half. Roll out each half to a 6" x 8" rectangle. Spread each rectangle with Coffee-Sugar Filling to about 1/2 inch of edges. Starting with long side, roll up like a jelly roll. Press ends together as you roll dough and press long side seam to seal. Press loaves seam-side down on an ungreased baking sheet. Form into crescent shapes. Cover and let rise in a warm place until doubled in bulk. Preheat oven to 350°F (175°C). Bake 30 to 35 minutes. Cool on rack. Prepare Brown Sugar Glaze. Brush on loaves. Makes 2 loaves.

Coffee-Sugar Filling:
Combine all ingredients in a small bowl. Blend well.
Brown Sugar Glaze:
Combine all ingredients in a small saucepan. Stir over low heat until smooth. Use while warm.

Swedish Christmas Coffeecake

Serve on Christmas morning with mugs of steaming hot coffee.

2 envelopes active dry yeast
1/2 cup warm water (110°F, 45°C)
1 teaspoon sugar
1/2 cup milk
1/2 cup butter or margarine (1 stick),
    room temperature
3/4 cup sugar
3 tablespoons instant coffee powder
1 teaspoon salt

1 egg, slightly beaten
About 5 cups all-purpose flour
1 cup minced candied fruit
4 tablespoons more sugar
4 tablespoons more butter or margarine
    room temperature
Confectioners Glaze, if desired, see below
Candied fruit for garnish

Confectioner's Glaze:
1 cup powdered sugar
1/2 teaspoon vanilla extract

2 tablespoons milk

Combine yeast, warm water and 1 teaspoon sugar. Let stand 5 minutes. In a small saucepan, heat milk to scalding or just below boiling, about 180°F (80°C). In a large bowl, combine scalded milk, 1/2 cup butter or margarine, 3/4 cup sugar, instant coffee powder and salt. Blend well. Add yeast mixture and egg. Blend well again. Stir in 2 cups flour. Beat until batter is very smooth and thick. Add enough flour, a small amount at a time, to form a stiff dough. On a lightly floured surface, knead until satiny smooth and elastic. Generously butter a large bowl. Place dough in bowl; turn to coat with butter. Cover and let rise in a warm place until doubled in bulk. Punch down and let stand 5 to 10 minutes. Lighly butter a large baking sheet; set aside. On a lightly floured surface, divide dough in half. Form into 2 balls. Roll out each ball into a 12-1/2-inch circle. Spread each circle with 2 tablespoons butter or margarine. Sprinkle equally with minced candied fruit and 4 tablespoons sugar. Roll up and curve to form 2 crescents. Place on prepared baking sheet. With a sharp knife, cut gashes along outside of each loaf at even intervals. Cover and let rise in a warm place until doubled in bulk. Preheat oven to 375°F (190°C). Bake 30 to 40 minutes. Cool on rack. If desired, drizzle with Confectioner's Glaze and sprinkle with candied fruit. Makes 2 loaves.

Confectioner's Glaze:
In a small bowl, combine powdered sugar, vanilla extract and milk. Blend well.

If you are mixing dissolved yeast with another liquid, such as scalded milk, make sure the other liquid has cooled to lukewarm. A few drops on the inside of your wrist should feel neither warm nor cool.

Walnut Loaf

You'll enjoy the nut coating and the moist texture.

2 teaspoons butter, softened
3 tablespoons ground walnuts
1/2 cup milk
2 tablespoons instant coffee powder
1-3/4 cups cake flour
1/4 teaspoon salt
1 teaspoon baking powder
1/2 cup butter or margarine (1 stick),
   room temperature

1 cup sugar
2 eggs
2 tablespoons butter or margarine,
   melted
3 tablespoons sugar
1 teaspoon instant coffee powder
1/2 cup chopped walnuts

Preheat oven to 350°F (175°C). Generously coat a 9" x 5" loaf pan with 2 teaspoons butter. Sprinkle with ground walnuts and rotate pan to coat evenly; set aside. In a small saucepan, heat milk to scalding or just below boiling, about 180°F (80°C). Stir in 2 tablespoons instant coffee powder. Remove from heat and cool to room temperature. Sift together cake flour, salt and baking powder. In a large bowl, cream butter or margarine with 1 cup sugar. Add eggs. Beat until light and fluffy. Add flour mixture alternately with milk-coffee mixture starting with flour mixture; stir to blend after each addition. Spoon into prepared pan. Pour 2 tablespoons melted butter or margarine over batter. Mix together 3 tablespoons sugar, 1 teaspoon instant coffee powder and chopped walnuts. Sprinkle evenly over loaf. Bake in preheated oven 45 to 50 minutes or until firm. Makes 1 loaf.

North Carolina's Best Muffins

Pumpkin pie spice joins coffee in a flavorful muffin.

1-1/3 cups all-purpose flour
2 tablespoons instant nonfat dry milk powder
4 teaspoons baking powder
1/2 teaspoon pumpkin pie spice
1/2 teaspoon salt
1 cup prepared hot coffee

2 tablespoons butter or margarine,
   room temperature
3/4 cup uncooked oatmeal
1 egg
1/4 cup sugar

Preheat oven to 400°F (205°C). Coat 12 muffin cups with vegetable shortening; set aside. Sift together flour, dry milk powder, baking powder, pumpkin pie spice and salt; set aside. Pour hot coffee over butter or margarine. Stir in oatmeal. Let stand 5 minutes. Stir in egg and sugar. Add sifted flour mixture; stir just enough to blend. Fill prepared muffin cups 3/4 full. Bake in preheated oven 20 to 25 minutes. Makes 12 muffins.

The secret of making quick breads, such as muffins, cornbread or pancakes, is not to overmix. The batter will be somewhat lumpy but these lumps disappear in the baking. Overmixing makes quick breads tough.

Honey-Nut Muffins

Delicious and nutritious!

1 cup all-purpose flour
1/2 teaspoon baking soda
1/2 teaspoon salt
1/4 teaspoon cinnamon
2 cups bran
3/4 cup milk

3/4 cup prepared hot coffee
2 tablespoons butter or margarine,
    room temperature
1/2 cup honey
1/2 cup chopped walnuts
1/2 cup raisins

Preheat oven to 425°F (220°C). Coat 12 muffin cups with vegetable shortening; set aside. Sift together flour, baking soda, salt and cinnamon into a large bowl. Stir in bran. In a small saucepan, heat milk to scalding or just below boiling, about 180°F (80°C). Add hot coffee, butter or margarine and honey. Stir until butter melts and mixture is blended. Pour over flour-bran mixture. Stir quickly to blend. Fold in walnuts and raisins. Fill prepared muffin cups 3/4 full. Bake in preheated oven 25 to 30 minutes. Makes 12 muffins.

How To Make Honey-Nut Muffins

1/Add hot coffee, butter or margarine and honey to scalded milk. Mix well. Stir quickly into flour-bran mixture. Add walnuts and raisins.

2/Fill prepared muffin cups only 3/4 full. Bake in preheated oven 25 to 30 minutes.

Rancher's Corn Bread

Bacon and coffee blend to make a delicious quick bread.

1 teaspoon vinegar	1 teaspoon baking powder
3/4 cup milk, room temperature	1/2 teaspoon baking soda
4 slices bacon	3/4 cup prepared coffee, room temperature
1 cup yellow cornmeal	1 egg
1 cup all-purpose flour	

Stir vinegar into milk; set aside. In a heavy 9- to 10-inch skillet, cook bacon over low heat until all fat is rendered and bacon is crisp. Drain bacon on paper towels and crumble; set aside. Preheat oven to 450°F (230°C). Pour all but a thin film of drippings into a measuring cup. Discard all but 1/4 cup drippings; set aside. Place skillet over low heat. In a medium bowl, combine cornmeal, flour, baking powder and baking soda. Make a well in the center. Pour milk-vinegar mixture into well. Add coffee and egg. Blend with a fork. Add reserved drippings and crumbled bacon. Blend well but quickly. Pour into heated skillet. Bake in preheated oven 20 to 25 minutes or until firm and lightly browned on top. Cut into wedges. Makes 6 to 8 servings.

Great Griddle Cakes

Top with Maple-Coffee Syrup and serve with crisp bacon for a fabulous breakfast.

1-1/2 cups pancake mix	1 egg
1/2 cup prepared coffee	1 tablespoon butter or margarine, melted
1/2 cup milk	Maple-Coffee Syrup, see below

Maple-Coffee Syrup

1 cup maple syrup	2 tablespoons butter or margarine,
1/4 cup prepared coffee	room temperature

Combine pancake mix, coffee, milk, egg and melted butter or margarine in a medium bowl. Blend until fairly smooth. Do not overmix. Lightly butter griddle and heat to almost sizzling. Drop batter by spoonfuls on hot griddle. Cook until bubbles form on surface. Turn to brown other side. Keep hot in warm oven. Prepare Maple-Coffee Syrup. Serve over griddle cakes. Makes 12 to 14 griddle cakes.

Maple-Coffee Syrup:
In a small saucepan, combine syrup, coffee and butter or margarine. Heat until butter or margarine melts and mixture is steaming. Serve warm. Makes about 1-1/4 cups syrup.

To lightly flour a surface, use about 1 tablespoon flour for each cup of flour called for in the recipe.

How To Make Rancher's Corn Bread

1/Cook bacon slowly until crisp, turning frequently. Drain on paper towels. Crumble and set aside.

2/Make a well in the center of the dry ingredients. Place the milk-vinegar mixture, egg and coffee in the well. Blend with a fork before adding the crumbled bacon and reserved drippings.

3/Blend well then quickly pour into hot skillet and bake in preheated oven.

Coffee-Can Date-Nut Bread

Spread with cream cheese for a tasty sandwich.

2 tablespoons butter, softened
4 tablespoons fine dry breadcrumbs
1 cup chopped dates
1 cup chopped pecans
1 cup prepared hot strong coffee
2 cups sifted all-prupose flour

1/2 teaspoon salt
1 teaspoon baking soda
4 tablespoons butter or margarine, softened
3/4 cup light brown sugar, firmly packed
1 egg
1/4 cup light rum or more prepared coffee

Generously butter insides of 2 (1-lb.) coffee cans with 2 tablespoons butter. Place 2 tablespoons breadcrumbs in each can. Cover with plastic lid or aluminum foil and shake vigorously to distribute crumbs evenly on bottoms and sides of cans; set cans aside. Combine dates and pecans in a small bowl. Pour hot coffee over and cool to lukewarm. Sift together flour, salt and baking soda. In a large bowl, cream 4 tablespoons butter or margarine with brown sugar until light and fluffy. Add egg. Beat well. Add flour mixture alternately with fruit-nut mixture, beating well after each addition. Stir in rum or 1/4 cup coffee. Spoon into prepared coffee cans, filling each can about half full. Cover top of can with foil; secure with a rubber band. Place a rack over simmering water in a large pot that allows some space between top of cans and pot lid. Place cans on rack. Cover and steam over medium heat, maintaining water at simmering 1 hour or until bread is firm and knife inserted in center comes out clean. To unmold, hold can upside down over rack and open bottom with a can opener; bread will slide out easily. Cool on rack before slicing. Makes 2 small loaves.

Orange Loaf

Fruit, coffee and nuts make an exquisite bread.

1 cup all-purpose flour
1 cup stone-ground whole-wheat flour
1 teaspoon baking powder
1 teaspoon baking soda
1/2 teaspoon salt
1 thick-skinned orange
1 cup raisins

About 1/2 cup prepared hot coffee
4 tablespoons butter or margarine,
    room temperature
1 cup sugar
1 egg
1/2 cup chopped walnuts

Preheat oven to 325°F (165°C). Oil a 10" x 6" loaf pan; set aside. Sift together all-purpose flour, whole-wheat flour, baking powder, baking soda and salt; set aside. Grate peel from orange. Cut orange in half and squeeze juice. In a measuring cup combine grated orange peel, juice and raisins. Add hot coffee to make 1 cup. Cool to room temperature. In a large bowl, cream butter or margarine with sugar. Add egg. Beat until light and fluffy. Add flour mixture alternately with orange-coffee mixture, stirring after each addition. Fold in nuts. Pour into prepared pan. Bake in pre-heated oven about 1 hour or until firm and lightly browned on top. Cool in pan on rack. Makes 1 loaf.

Gelatin Desserts

If you think of gelatin desserts as plain fare, think again, and think coffee. From Classic Coffee Gelatin topped with Sweetened Whipped Cream to delectable Almond Mousse, coffee gelatins are extraordinary desserts. You can work wonders with a freshly made full-bodied brew and unflavored gelatin. Cubed or whipped, layered or plain, coffee gelatins are easy to make, delicious and beautiful. They have that made-for-the-occasion look that transforms the simplest of meals into a party or turns a casual get-together into a festive occasion.

All the coffee gelatins included here are easy to make but there are a few basics that guarantee success every time.

• For a clear, uniformly set mold, gelatin must be completely dissolved.

• Use freshly made, strong coffee for true deep-down flavor. Leftover coffee may be stale and instant does not give the coffee essence that makes this delicious difference.

• Refrigerate until ready to serve. When you plan a molded coffee dessert for a buffet party, unmold it and place it on the table just before dessert is served. Firm gelatin molds hold up well for as long as half an hour, but after that they begin to weep.

• To unmold gelatin easily, dip mold briefly in quite warm, but not hot, water and loosen the edges with a blunt knife. Shake the mold slightly to see if the gelatin has loosened. Rinse the serving plate in cold water to prevent breaking the mold when you slide it into place. Place the rinsed plate upside down on top of the mold and invert. The pan should pull off easily and you can ease the gelatin into position on the wet serving plate.

Some of these recipes suggest piling the gelatin in individual dessert glasses. Here's your chance to use the elegant glassware that's been hiding in the back of the cupboard. Brandy snifters or bubble-shaped wine glasses make a plain dessert festive and elegant. Use your imagination and try everything you've got!

Easy Prepare-Ahead Dinner

Jamaican Stuffed Peppers, page 26
Tiny Steamed Onions &
Green Beans With Pimiento
Classic Coffee Gelatin, page 50
Café à l'Orange, page 152

Classic Coffee Gelatin

The perfect ending to a substantial dinner.

2 envelopes unflavored gelatin
1/2 cup sugar
1 cup prepared hot coffee

2 cups prepared cold coffee
Sweetened Whipped Cream, page 122,
   if desired

Combine gelatin and sugar in a medium bowl. Add hot coffee. Stir until gelatin and sugar dissolve. Stir in cold coffee. Pour into 4 to 6 dessert glasses. Refrigerate until firm. If desired, garnish with Sweetened Whipped Cream. Makes 4 to 6 servings.

Variation

Spirited Gelatin: Substitute 1/4 to 1/2 cup brandy, rum or sherry for 1/4 to 1/2 cup cold coffee.

Jellied Coffee & Cream

A beautiful and easy parfait.

2 envelopes unflavored gelatin
1/2 cup sugar
2 tablespooons instant coffee powder
1 cup almost boiling water

1 cup cold water
1/2 cup brandy
1 pint coffee ice cream, slightly softened

Combine gelatin, sugar and instant coffee powder in blender container. Add almost boiling water. Blend until gelatin dissolves. Measure 1/2 cup gelatin mixture into a large bowl; set aside. Add cold water and brandy to remaining gelatin mixture. Pour into an 8- or 9-inch square baking dish. Refrigerate about 30 minutes until thickened. Blend half the softened ice cream into reserved gelatin mixture. Spoon thickened clear coffee gelatin into dessert glasses. Top with ice cream mixture. Refrigerate about 30 minutes. Just before serving, top with remaining ice cream. Makes 4 or 5 servings.

To make gelatin with fruit or nut pattern on top, chill a thin layer of gelatin in mold until thick. Chill remaining gelatin until syrupy. Place fruit or nuts on thickened gelatin in mold; top with thin layer of syrupy gelatin. Chill until firm; fill mold with remaining gelatin. Chill to set.

Rum-Coffee Charlotte

Can anyone resist coffee and chocolate?

1/2 cup prepared cold coffee
3 envelopes unflavored gelatin
5 egg yolks
3/4 cup sugar
1 cup more prepared cold coffee
1/4 cup light rum or
   1 teaspoon imitation rum flavoring

1/2 pint whipping cream
18 to 24 chocolate cookie wafers,
   each broken into 3 or 4 pieces
Sweetened Whipped Cream, page 122,
   if desired
Chocolate cookie crumbs, if desired

Lightly butter a 6-cup ring mold; set aside. Place 1/2 cup cold coffee in a small bowl. Sprinkle with gelatin. Let stand 5 minutes to soften. Combine egg yolks and sugar in top of double boiler over, not in, simmering water. Beat until mixture thickens to a custard and triples its original volume. Add softened gelatin. Stir until dissolved. Add 1 cup cold coffee and rum or rum flavoring; mix well. Cool custard to room temperature. In a large bowl, beat whipping cream until stiff. Beat custard again to blend; fold into whipped cream. Pour about 1/3 of the custard into prepared mold. Cover with about half the chocolate wafer pieces. Repeat with another 1/3 of custard mixture and remaining chocolate wafer pieces. Top with remaining custard. Refrigerate until firm. Just before serving, unmold and cut in thick slices. If desired, top each serving with a dab of Sweetened Whipped Cream and sprinkle with chocolate cookie crumbs. Makes 6 to 8 servings.

Pineapple Cup

Pineapple gives a tropical touch to a cool summer dessert.

1-1/2 envelopes unflavored gelatin
1/4 cup sugar
1 cup prepared hot coffee
1 (8-oz.) can sliced pineapple in syrup

1/4 cup light rum or
   1 teaspoon imitation rum flavoring
1-1/4 to 1-1/2 cups prepared cold coffee
Dairy sour cream

Combine gelatin and sugar in a bowl. Add 1 cup hot coffee. Stir until gelatin dissolves. Drain syrup from pineapple and measure. Add rum or rum flavoring and enough cold coffee to measure 2 cups liquid. Add to gelatin mixture. Refrigerate until thickened but not set. Spoon about 3/4 gelatin equally into 4 stemmed glasses. Top each with 1 pineapple slice. Cover with remaining gelatin. Refrigerate until firm. Just before serving, top with sour cream. Makes 4 servings.

1/Use a small sharp knife to cut 2 concentric circles around the surface of the gelatin.

2/With a sharp-edged spoon, scoop out the gelatin between the circles, making a 1-inch deep channel. Prepare Gelatin Topping with scooped out gelatin.

How To Make Lemon Cream Ring Mold

4/Cover entire surface of mold and filling with Gelatin Topping. Refrigerate mold until very firm. To serve, unmold onto serving plate and fill center with stiffly beaten Lemon Cream Filling.

3/Fill channel with Lemon Cream Filling containing gelatin.

Lemon Cream Ring Mold

Looks fabulous and tastes delicious.

1 cup prepared cold coffee

3 envelopes unflavored gelatin

1 cup prepared hot coffee

3/4 cup granulated sugar

3 cups more prepared cold coffee

1/2 cup light rum or more prepared cold coffee

Gelatin Topping, see below

Lemon Cream Fillings, see below

Gelatin Topping:

Reserved gelatin scooped from mold

Lemon Cream Fillings:

1 pint whipping cream

3/4 cup powdered sugar

2 tablespoons grated lemon peel

1 teaspoon lemon extract

1/4 cup cold water

1 envelope unflavored gelatin

Place 1 cup cold coffee in a large saucepan. Sprinkle with 3 envelopes gelatin. Let stand 5 minutes to soften. Add hot coffee and granulated sugar. Stir over low heat until gelatin and sugar dissolve. Remove from heat. Add 3 cups cold coffee and rum or 1/2 cup cold coffee. Rinse a 6-cup ring mold with cold water. Pour mixture into wet mold. Refrigerate until very firm. With a small sharp knife, cut a ring around the top of gelatin about 1-inch deep and 3/4 inch from side of mold. Repeat with a second ring 3/4 inch from center of mold. With a small sharp-edged spoon, scoop out gelatin between inner and outer rings baking a 1-inch deep indentation around top of gelatin. Return mold to refrigerator. Prepare Gelatin Topping with scooped out gelatin. Prepare Lemon Cream Fillings. Fill scooped-out ring in coffee gelatin with Lemon Cream Filling containing gelatin. Cover entire surface evenly with Gelatin Topping. Refrigerate until very firm. Just before serving, unmold onto serving plate. Fill center with chilled, stiffly beaten Lemon Cream Filling. Makes 8 to 10 servings.

Gelatin Topping:

Place scooped out gelatin in a small saucepan over low heat until melted. Refrigerate until thickened and cold.

Lemon Cream Fillings:

In a small bowl, beat whipping cream until thickened but not stiff. Fold in powdered sugar, grated lemon peel and lemon extract. Spoon half of whipped cream into another bowl and beat until stiff. Refrigerate until serving time. Set aside remaining thickened whipped cream. Place cold water in a small saucepan. Sprinkle with 1 envelope gelatin. Stir over low heat until gelatin dissolves. Fold into thickened whipped cream. There are now 2 bowls of whipped cream filling: one has no gelatin, has been beaten until stiff, then refrigerated; the other is thickened and contains gelatin.

Macaroon Bavarian

Macaroons, whipped cream and ice cream blended into sweetened coffee gelatin.

1/2 cup cold water
2 envelopes unflavored gelatin
2 cups prepared hot coffee
1/2 cup sugar

1 pint coffee ice cream, softened
1/2 pint whipping cream
1 cup fine dry macaroon crumbs
Macaroon crumbs for garnish

Place cold water in a medium saucepan. Sprinkle with gelatin. Let stand 5 minutes to soften. Add hot coffee. Stir over low heat until gelatin dissolves. Stir in sugar until dissolved. Remove from heat. Pour into a large bowl. Add ice cream about 2 tablespoons at a time, stirring until ice cream melts. Refrigerate until mixture begins to thicken. Beat cream until stiff. Fold into coffee mixture. Fold in 1 cup macaroon crumbs. Refrigerate until thickened. Pile high in 8 to 10 sherbet glasses. Refrigerate until serving time. Garnish with macaroon crumbs, if desired. Makes 8 to 10 servings.

Apricot Cream

Velvety smooth with a fresh fruit taste.

1 (3-1/2-oz.) pkg. apricot-flavored gelatin
1-1/2 cups prepared hot coffee
1/2 cup syrup from 1 (1-lb.) can apricot
   halves; reserve halves and 1/4 cup more
   syrup

1/2 cup dairy sour cream
Glazed Apricot Halves, see below

Glazed Apricot Halves:
1/4 cup reserved apricot syrup
1 cup sugar

Reserved apricot halves

In a medium bowl, combine gelatin and hot coffee. Stir until gelatin dissolves. Add 1/2 cup apricot syrup and sour cream. Mix well. Chill until thickened. Beat with rotary beater until fluffy. Rinse a 4-cup mold with cold water. Pour gelatin-apricot mixture into wet mold. Refrigerate until very firm. Prepare Glazed Apricot Halves. Just before serving, unmold gelatin onto serving platter. Garnish with Glazed Apricot Halves. Makes 4 to 6 servings.

Glazed Apricot Halves:
Combine reserved apricot syrup and sugar in a medium saucepan. Simmer until sugar dissolves and syrup thickens, stirring occasionally. Add apricot halves. Simmer 5 minutes. Chill.

Mandarin Mold

After a Chinese dinner, serve this handsome dessert with fortune cookies.

2 envelopes unflavored gelatin	1 (14-oz.) can sweetened condensed milk
1 cup water	1/2 cup shredded coconut
3 tablespoons frozen orange juice concentrate	Tangerine Sauce, see below
1 cup prepared coffee	

Tangerine Sauce:

2 cups water	3 tablespoons frozen orange juice concentrate
1 cup sugar	2 teaspoons cornstarch,
2 tangerines, peeled and sectioned,	dissolved in 1 tablespoon water
white pith removed	3 teaspoons instant coffee powder

Sprinkle gelatin over 2 tablespoons water. Let stand 5 minutes to soften. In a medium saucepan, bring remaining water to a boil. Dissolve softened gelatin in boiling water. Stir in orange juice concentrate and coffee. Remove from heat. Add condensed milk. Mix well. Refrigerate until thickened. Beat until fluffy. Stir in coconut. Rinse a 6-cup ring mold with cold water. Pour gelatin mixture into wet mold. Refrigerate until firm. Prepare Tangerine Sauce. To serve, dip bottom of mold briefly in warm but not hot water; loosen sides with a flat knife and unmold onto serving platter. Decorate with tangerine slices from sauce. Serve sauce separately. Makes 6 to 8 servings.

Tangerine Sauce:
Combine water, sugar, tangerine sections and orange juice concentrate in a medium saucepan. Bring to a boil. Lower heat and simmer until tangerine sections are tender. Remove tangerine sections with a slotted spoon; set aside. Stir in dissolved cornstarch. Cook over medium heat until thickened and clear. Remove from heat. Stir in instant coffee powder. Return tangerine sections to sauce. Chill. Makes about 1-1/2 cups sauce.

Jellied Irish Coffee

Brew fresh coffee and use the best imported Irish whiskey.

1/2 cup prepared cold coffee	1/3 cup light brown sugar, firmly packed
1 envelope unflavored gelatin	1/2 cup imported Irish whiskey
1-1/2 cups prepared hot coffee	1/2 cup whipping cream

Place cold coffee in a small saucepan. Sprinkle with gelatin; let stand 5 minutes to soften. Add hot coffee and brown sugar. Stir over low heat until sugar and gelatin dissolve. Cool to room temperature. Add whiskey. Fill 4 Irish Coffee glasses, heavy-stemmed glasses, brandy snifters or Old Fashioned glasses about 3/4 full. Refrigerate until set. Whip cream with a wire whisk or fork until thickened but not stiff. Just before serving, top with whipped cream. Makes 4 servings.

Pistachio Charlotte

Pistachio-yogurt pudding on bottom; coffee gelatin on the top.

1/4 cup prepared cold coffee
1 envelope unflavored gelatin
3/4 cup prepared hot coffee
1/4 cup light brown sugar, firmly packed
2 tablespoons brandy or
   1 teaspoon imitation brandy flavoring
12 lady fingers

1-1/2 cups cold milk
1 (3-3/4-oz.) pkg. pistachio instant pudding
   and pie filling mix
1 (8-oz.) carton vanilla yogurt
Sweetened Whipped Cream, page 122
   for garnish
Instant coffee powder for garnish

Place cold coffee in a small bowl. Sprinkle with gelatin. Let stand 5 minutes to soften. Add hot coffee and brown sugar. Stir until gelatin and sugar dissolve. Stir in brandy or brandy flavoring. Refrigerate until thickened. Split lady fingers and cut in half crosswise. Line sides and bottom of an 8-inch springform pan with lady fingers. Combine milk and pudding mix in a small deep bowl. Beat slowly about 1 minute to blend. Add yogurt and mix well. Pour into prepared pan. Pour thickened coffee gelatin over pudding. Refrigerate until gelatin is firm. Just before serving, top with Sweetened Whipped Cream and sprinkle lightly with instant coffee powder. Makes 6 to 8 servings.

Marshmallow-Pineapple Mold

Easy, inexpensive and delicious.

2 envelopes unflavored gelatin
4 tablespoons cold water
2 cups prepared hot coffee
8 to 10 marshmallows

1 cup pineapple juice
1 (8-oz.) can crushed pineapple, undrained
Sweetened Whipped Cream, page 122,
   if desired

Sprinkle gelatin over cold water. Let stand 5 minutes to soften. Place hot coffee in a medium saucepan. Add softened gelatin. Stir until dissolved. Add marshmallows. Place over low heat until marshmallows melt; do not boil. Add 1 cup pineapple juice to gelatin-marshmallow mixture. Refrigerate until thickened. Beat with rotary beater until fluffy. Fold in undrained crushed pineapple. Rinse a 6-cup mold with cold water. Pour mixture into wet mold. Refrigerate until firm. Just before serving, unmold onto serving platter. Garnish with Sweetened Whipped Cream, if desired. Makes 6 to 8 servings.

It takes 20 to 45 minutes in most refrigerators for gelatin to reach the thickened and syrupy stage needed for stirring in fruit or whipped cream.

Caramel Cream

Delicious and rich—but easy on your budget.

1 envelope unflavored gelatin
1/4 cup cold water
1/2 cup sugar
1/2 cup prepared hot coffee

1/2 cup more sugar
1 teaspoon vanilla extract
1/2 pint whipping cream
Maraschino cherries and juice, if desired

Sprinkle gelatin over cold water. Let stand 5 minutes to soften. Place 1/2 cup sugar in a heavy skillet. Stir over low heat to a light golden syrup. Add hot coffee. Stir until smooth. Remove from heat. Stir in softened gelatin, 1/2 cup sugar and vanilla extract. Mix well. Pour into a large bowl. Refrigerate until thickened. Beat whipping cream until stiff. Fold into thickened gelatin. Rinse a 4-cup decorative mold with cold water. Pour gelatin mixture into wet mold. Refrigerate until firm. Just before serving, unmold and garnish with maraschino cherries and a little cherry juice, if desired. Makes 6 to 8 servings.

Coconut Cream

Toasted coconut gives this easy dessert its special flavor.

1 cup shredded coconut
1/2 cup prepared cold coffee
2 envelopes unflavored gelatin
1-1/2 cups prepared hot coffee

1/2 cup sugar
1/2 pint whipping cream
Sweetened Whipped Cream, page 122,
    if desired

Preheat oven to 350°F (175°C). Spread coconut on a baking sheet. Toast in preheated oven about 15 minutes until golden and crisp, stirring often. Cool. Place cold coffee in a large bowl. Sprinkle with gelatin. Let stand 5 minutes to soften. Add hot coffee and sugar. Stir until gelatin and sugar dissolve. Refrigerate until thickened. Stir in toasted coconut. Whip cream until stiff. Fold into gelatin. Chill. Serve in sherbet or parfait glasses. If desired, garnish with Sweetened Whipped Cream. Makes 6 to 8 servings.

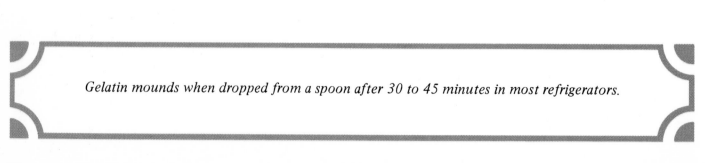

Gelatin mounds when dropped from a spoon after 30 to 45 minutes in most refrigerators.

Peach Party Mold

Superb raspberry sauce over coffee-flavored peaches and cream.

2 envelopes unflavored gelatin
1/2 cup boiling water
2 tablespoons instant coffee powder
1/4 cup brandy or 2 teaspoons imitation
   brandy flavoring plus 3 tablespoons water

1 (10-oz.) pkg. frozen peaches, thawed
1/2 cup sugar
4 eggs
1/2 pint whipping cream
Raspberry Sauce, see below

Raspberry Sauce:
1 (10-oz.) pkg. frozen raspberries, thawed
2 tablespoons cornstarch

1 tablespoon brandy or 1/2 teaspoon imitation
   brandy flavoring plus 2-1/2 teaspoons water

Place gelatin in blender container. Pour in boiling water; blend on high speed until smooth. Add instant coffee powder and brandy or brandy flavoring plus water. Blend until coffee dissolves. Add peaches and sugar. Blend to a puree. In a large bowl, beat eggs until very light. Add peach puree. Blend well. Place bowl in a large pan of ice and water. Stir until mixture mounds when dropped from a spoon. Or refrigerate until thickened, stirring frequently for a smooth texture. Remove from ice water or refrigerator. In a large bowl, whip cream until stiff. Fold in thickened peach mixture. Rinse a 6-cup decorative mold with cold water. Pour mixture into wet mold. Refrigerate several hours or overnight. Unmold and serve with Raspberry Sauce. Makes 8 to 10 servings.

Raspberry Sauce:
In a small saucepan, heat raspberries in their liquid until bubbly. Dissolve cornstarch in brandy or brandy flavoring plus water and 1 tablespoon juice from raspberries. Add to raspberries. Cook and stir until thickened. Chill before serving.

Peppermint Parfaits

Everybody loves peppermint candy and coffee in ice cream.

1-1/2 cups prepared coffee
2 envelopes unflavored gelatin
1/2 cup finely crushed hard peppermint candy
1 pint coffee ice cream, slightly softened

1/2 pint whipping cream
1/4 cup more finely crushed hard peppermint
   candy

Place coffee in a small heavy saucepan. Sprinkle with gelatin. Let stand 5 minutes to soften. Add 1/2 cup crushed peppermint candy. Stir over low heat until gelatin dissolves and candy melts. Remove from heat. Add softened ice cream a few tablespoons at a time, stirring until blended. Refrigerate until thickened. In a large bowl, whip cream until stiff. Just before serving, fold ice cream mixture into whipped cream. Spoon into 8 dessert glasses or a 2-quart serving bowl. Sprinkle with 1/4 cup crushed peppermint candy. Makes 8 servings.

Almond Mousse

Almonds, coffee gelatin and whipped cream in long-stemmed elegance.

1 (2-1/2-oz.) pkg. slivered almonds
1/4 cup cold water
1 envelope unflavored gelatin
1 cup sugar
1/2 cup water

1-1/2 cups prepared coffee
1/2 pint whipping cream
2 tablespoons almond liqueur or
    1/2 teaspoon almond extract
Whole almonds for garnish

Spread almonds on a baking sheet. Place under broiler heat 2 to 4 minutes until lightly toasted. Stir once or twice and watch closely to prevent burning. Set aside. Place 1/4 cup cold water in a small bowl. Sprinkle with gelatin. Let stand 5 minutes to soften. In a small saucepan, combine sugar and 1/2 cup water. Stir over low heat until sugar dissolves. Bring to a full boil; boil 2 to 3 minutes. Remove from heat and stir in softened gelatin until dissolved. Stir in coffee. Refrigerate until mixture begins to thicken. In a large bowl, whip cream until stiff. Fold in gelatin mixture, toasted almonds and almond liqueur or extract. Refrigerate until serving time. Pile high in stemmed glasses. Top each serving with a whole almond. Makes 8 to 10 servings.

Chocolate Icebox Cake

A longtime favorite with a new coffee flavor.

3 eggs
2 (1-oz.) squares unsweetened chocolate
3/4 cup prepared coffee
2 envelopes unflavored gelatin
1/3 cup water

1/3 cup sugar
16 shortbread cookies, crumbled (2-1/2 cups)
Sweetened Whipped Cream, page 122
    for garnish

Separate eggs; set aside to bring to room temperature. Place chocolate and coffee in a small saucepan over low heat until chocolate melts. Sprinkle gelatin over water; let stand 5 minutes to soften. Add gelatin mixture and sugar to chocolate-coffee mixture. Stir until dissolved; do not boil. Stir in egg yolks. Continue stirring over low heat 2 to 3 minutes. In a medium bowl, beat egg whites until stiff. Fold in chocolate-coffee mixture then crumbled cookies. Rinse a 4-cup mold with cold water. Spoon mixture into wet mold. Refrigerate several hours. Just before serving, turn out onto serving dish. Garnish with Sweetened Whipped Cream. Makes 6 to 8 servings.

The firmness gelatin requires for unmolding and serving is reached in 4 to 5 hours or longer.

Custards & Puddings

Few desserts are more certain of success than custards and puddings. And coffee, like fine brandy, gives a new and delicious aura to longtime favorites like Floating Island and Indian Pudding Congolese. That's only the beginning. Maple-Rum Pots de Crème, pronounced *poh-da-crem*, please the most knowledgeable gourmets. Brandy Snifter Pudding is an original dessert for an elegant dinner. For heartier fare, try Kentucky Puddin', a sweet-potato recipe from a talented country cook.

Many of these recipes call for custards or puddings made from scratch; others use the convenient packaged pudding mixes. Both are good, but be sure to try your hand at making a few boiled and baked custards. They require less skill and time than you think. The first thing to remember is that all custards, boiled—which are really never boiled at all—or baked, require gentle heat. Make boiled custards in the top of a double boiler over, not in, simmering water. Set baked custards and pots de crème in a long shallow baking pan on top of a folded paper towel. This prevents the cups from shifting. Pour hot water into the pan to come about halfway up the sides of the cups.

Steamed puddings, such as Holiday Mincemeat Pudding, are greatly enhanced by soaking in a mixture of half coffee and half brandy. Wrap first in cheesecloth then in aluminum foil. Let the pudding mellow at least a week. Reheat it on a rack in a covered pot over steaming water. Your steamed pudding will make a dramatic entrance if you pour a tablespoon or so of warm brandy over it, carefully ignite the brandy and carry the pudding to the table aflame with holiday spirits!

Patio Luncheon

Chili Dip With Taco Chips
Easy Empanadas, page 28
Avocado & Tomato Salad
Cajeta de Cafe, page 66
Cinnamon Cafe con Leche, page 17

Lemon-Coffee Cream

Quick and easy new dessert with vanilla pudding mix.

1 (3-3/4-oz.) pkg. vanilla pudding
   and pie filling mix
1/3 cup sugar
2 egg yolks
2-1/4 cups water
1 tablespoon fresh lemon juice

1/2 teaspoon grated lemon peel
1/2 cup prepared ice-cold coffee
1 pkg. whipped topping mix
2 tablespoons brandy or
   1 teaspoon imitation brandy flavoring
1/4 cup grated walnuts

Combine pudding mix and sugar in a medium saucepan. Place egg yolks and water in blender container. Blend well. Or beat egg yolks, add water and beat to blend well. Add to pudding mix and sugar. Stir over medium heat to a full boil. Pour about 1/4 of the pudding into a small bowl. Place plastic wrap directly on surface of pudding and set aside until cool. Add lemon juice and peel to remaining pudding. Pour into 4 to 6 dessert glasses. Place plastic wrap directly on surface of each pudding. Refrigerate until chilled. Combine cold coffee and whipped topping mix in a medium bowl. Beat until soft peaks form when beater is slowly lifted from bowl. Continue to beat until light and fluffy. Fold in reserved vanilla pudding and brandy or brandy flavoring. Spoon on top of each lemon pudding. Sprinkle with grated walnuts. Refrigerate several hours or until chilled. Makes 4 to 6 servings.

Koffee Klatch Bread Pudding

Tastes best while it's still warm.

1 (1-lb.) loaf French- or Italian-style bread
1/2 cup butter or margarine (1 stick)
   room temperature
1 tablespoon grated lemon peel
3/4 cup raisins
2 cups prepared hot coffee
1 cup brown sugar, firmly packed

2 eggs, well beaten
1/4 teaspoon cinnamon
1/2 teaspoon vanilla extract
1 tablespoon granulated sugar
Sweetened Whipped Cream, page 122,
   or vanilla ice cream

Preheat oven to 375°F (190°C). Butter a 9-inch square baking pan. Slice bread. Spread slices with butter or margarine. Cut into cubes. Place in a large bowl. Add lemon peel, raisins and coffee. Mix thoroughly. Let stand about 30 minutes. Add brown sugar, eggs, cinnamon and vanilla extract. Blend. Pour into prepared baking pan. Bake in preheated oven 1 hour or until knife inserted in center comes out clean. Sprinkle top evenly with granulated sugar. Place directly until broiler heat until glazed. Spoon into dessert dishes and top with Sweetened Whipped Cream or vanilla ice cream. Makes 8 to 10 servings.

Nesselrode Pots de Crème

Bottled Nesselrode sauce to make these delicacies is usually available in gourmet shops.

2 tablespoons instant coffee powder
1/2 cup hot water
4 egg yolks
1/2 pint whipping cream
1/2 cup sugar

1/2 teaspoon vanilla extract
6 teaspoons bottled Nesselrode sauce
Sweetened Whipped Cream, page 122,
  if desired
Candy coffee beans, if desired

Preheat oven to 350°F (175°C). Dissolve instant coffee powder in hot water; set aside. In a medium bowl, stir egg yolks only until mixed. Place cream in a large saucepan over low heat until steaming. Remove from heat. Add sugar and dissolved coffee powder. Stir until sugar dissolves. Very slowly pour over egg yolks, stirring constantly. Add vanilla extract. Stir to blend; do not beat or whip. Strain into a pitcher. Place 1 teaspoon Nesselrode sauce in each of 6 half-cup pot de crème or custard cups. Pour custard mixture into cups to about 1/4 inch of rim. With a spoon, skim any foam from tops. Place cups on paper towels in a long shallow baking pan. Pour hot water into pan halfway up outsides of cups. Bake on middle rack in preheated oven 45 minutes or until firm. Remove from hot water. Cool uncovered at room temperature. Cover and refrigerate until chilled. If desired, garnish with Sweetened Whipped Cream and candy coffee beans. Makes 6 servings.

Maple-Rum Pots de Crème

Little cups of creamy maple-rum custard laced with coffee.

1/2 pint whipping cream
1/2 cup light brown sugar, firmly packed
4 egg yolks
1/2 cup prepared cold coffee
1 teaspoon maple extract

1/4 cup light rum or
  1 teaspoon imitation rum flavoring plus
  1/4 cup coffee
Sweetened Whipped Cream, page 122, or
  dairy sour cream, if desired

Preheat oven to 350° (175°C). In a small saucepan, heat cream until bubbles appear around edges. Add brown sugar. Stir until dissolved. Remove from heat and cool slightly. In a medium bowl, stir egg yolks only until mixed. Stir in 1/2 cup coffee, maple extract and rum or rum flavoring plus 1/4 cup coffee. Strain into a pitcher. Place 6 half-cup pot de crème cups or custard cups on paper towels in a long shallow baking pan. Pour custard mixture into cups to about 1/4 inch of rim. Pour hot water into pan halfway up outside of cups. Bake on middle rack in preheated oven 40 to 45 minutes or until a knife inserted near center comes out clean. Cover and refrigerate until chilled. If desired, serve topped with Sweetened Whipped Cream or sour cream. Makes 6 servings.

Crème de Marrons Glacés

Marrons, imported from France, are a type of chestnut in syrup; look for them in gourmet shops.

1 (8-oz.) jar marrons glacés
4 egg yolks
2 tablespoons sugar

1/3 cup prepared coffee
1/2 cup whipping cream
Whipped cream, if desired

Drain marrons; reserve 1/3 cup syrup. Chop marrons coarsely and place in 6 to 8 dessert glasses. Cover each dish with plastic wrap and refrigerate. In top of double boiler, over, not in, simmering water, beat egg yolks with sugar until blended. Add reserved syrup from marrons, coffee and cream. Stir over simmering water until custard thickens and coats a wooden spoon. Cool. Place plastic wrap directly on surface of custard and refrigerate until chilled. To serve, spoon chilled custard over marrons. If desired, garnish with whipped cream. Makes 6 to 8 servings.

Cajeta de Cafe

This Latin American caramel custard creates its own sauce.

3/4 cup granulated sugar
4 whole eggs
2 egg yolks

1 (15-oz.) can condensed milk
1 cup prepared cold strong coffee
1/2 cup brown sugar, firmly packed

Preheat oven to 375°F (190°C). Place granulated sugar in a square or round flat-bottomed casserole that can be used over direct heat and in the oven. Stir over low heat until sugar dissolves to a golden syrup. Remove from heat. With pot holders, rotate casserole to coat bottom with caramelized sugar. Set aside until completely cool. Combine remaining ingredients in blender container; blend until smooth. Or place whole eggs and egg yolks in a medium bowl, beat until frothy, add remaining ingredients and beat until smooth. Pour into caramel-lined casserole. Place casserole in a large baking pan and pour in hot water about halfway up outside of casserole. Bake in preheated oven 1 hour or until a knife inserted near center comes out clean. Cool to room temperature. Refrigerate until chilled. Serve in dessert glasses; spoon some of the sauce from the bottom of the casserole over each serving. Makes 6 to 8 servings.

If your finished custard appears the least bit lumpy, beat it briefly with a wire whisk and it will smooth out quickly.

French Chocolate Mousse

With or without Mocha Cream, this dessert is sensational!

4 large eggs
4 (1-oz.) squares semisweet chocolate
2 tablespoons instant coffee powder
1/4 cup light rum or
   1 teaspoon imitation rum flavoring
   plus 1/4 cup whipping cream

Pinch salt
1/4 cup sugar
1/2 cup whipping cream
Mocha Cream, see below
1 (1-oz.) square semisweet chocolate, grated,
   if desired

Mocha Cream:
1/2 cup whipping cream
3 tablespoons powdered sugar

1 tablespoon instant coffee powder

Separate eggs while cold, placing whites in a large bowl and yolks in a small bowl. Bring to room temperature. Place chocolate, instant coffee powder and rum or rum flavoring plus 1/4 cup whipping cream in top of double boiler over, not in, simmering water until chocolate is almost melted. Remove from heat and stir until chocolate melts completely. Cool. Add egg yolks, salt and sugar. Beat until smooth. Beat whipping cream until stiff. Fold about 1/4 of the egg whites into chocolate mixture, then fold mixture into remaining whites. Fold in whipped cream. Pour into a serving bowl or individual dessert glasses. Cover and refrigerate until chilled. Prepare Mocha Cream. Just before serving, top mousse with Mocha Cream. If desired, sprinkle with grated chocolate. Makes 6 to 8 servings.

Mocha Cream:
In a small bowl, beat cream until thickened. Beat in powdered sugar and instant coffee powder; continue to beat to the consistency of a thick custard.

Swiss Chocolate Mousse

Orange and bittersweet chocolate blend with coffee for a delightful new taste.

4 eggs
1/2 cup sugar
2 (3-oz.) Swiss bittersweet chocolate bars,
   broken into squares
3 tablespoons instant coffee powder

1/4 cup Grand Marnier liqueur,
   other orange liqueur or
   freshly squeezed orange juice
1 tablespoon grated orange peel

Separate eggs while cold, placing yolks in a small bowl and whites in a medium bowl. Bring to room temperature. Blend sugar into egg yolks; set aside. In top of double boiler, combine chocolate, instant coffee powder and liqueur or orange juice. Place over, not in, simmering water until chocolate melts. Stir until smooth. Add orange peel. Beat egg yolk mixture until light and fluffy. Stir into chocolate mixture. Stir over low heat 3 to 4 minutes. Remove from heat and cool to room temperature. Beat egg whites until stiff. Fold in chocolate mixture. Spoon into 8 to 10 small dessert glasses or demitasse cups. Chill before serving. Makes 8 to 10 small servings.

How To Make
Torte of Many Layers

1/Press mixture of butter or margarine, chopped pecans and flour into baking pan. Bake and cool.

3/Spoon vanilla pudding mixture on top and, with a knife, spread over and into chocolate to create a marbled effect. Top with remaining whipped topping and chopped pecans. Refrigerate 8 hours or more.

2/Spread cream cheese mixture over baked layer. Cover with chocolate pudding mixture.

Torte of Many Layers

Here's a layered dessert so easy and delicious you'll make it again and again.

1/2 cup butter or margarine (1 stick)
1 cup chopped pecans
1 cup self-rising flour
2 envelopes whipped topping mix
1-1/2 cups cold milk
1 (8-oz.) pkg. cream cheese, room temperature
1 cup light brown sugar, firmly packed
1 (4-1/2-oz.) pkg. chocolate instant pudding
   and pie filling mix

1-1/2 cups prepared cold coffee
1 (3-3/4-oz.) pkg. vanilla instant pudding
   and pie filling mix
1-1/4 cups more cold milk
1/4 cup light rum or
   1 teaspoon imitation rum flavoring
   plus 1/4 cup milk
1/2 cup more chopped pecans

Preheat oven to 350°F (175°C). Melt butter or margarine in a medium skillet. Stir in 1 cup chopped pecans and self-rising flour. Blend well. Press into a 13" x 9" baking pan. Bake in preheated oven 15 minutes. Cool. Prepare whipped topping mix with 1-1/2 cups cold milk according to package directions. In a medium bowl, beat cream cheese with brown sugar until light and fluffy. Fold in half the prepared topping mix. Spread evenly on baked pecan-butter layer. Refrigerate remaining topping mix. Prepare chocolate instant pudding and pie filling using cold coffee instead of the liquid called for in the package directions. Spread over cream cheese layer. Prepare vanilla instant pudding and pie filling with 1-1/4 cups milk and rum or rum flavoring plus 1/4 cup milk according to package directions. Spread over chocolate layer using a knife for a marbled effect. Spoon remaining prepared topping mix over vanilla layer; spread evenly with 1/2 cup chopped pecans. Refrigerate 8 hours or longer. To serve, cut into squares. Makes 12 to 16 servings.

Mocha-Yogurt Dessert

Tangy yogurt joins coffee and instant pudding for a new taste experience.

1 (4-1/2-oz.) pkg. chocolate instant pudding
   and pie filling mix
1/2 cup prepared cold coffee

1-1/2 cups cold milk
1 (8-oz.) carton coffee-flavored yogurt
Toasted slivered almonds, if desired

In a medium bowl, combine pudding mix, coffee and milk. Beat with electric mixer on low speed about 2 minutes until blended. Fold in yogurt. Spoon into dessert glasses. Refrigerate until chilled. If desired, sprinkle with toasted slivered almonds before serving. Makes 4 to 5 servings.

Baked custards are cooked when a knife inserted in the center comes out clean. Remove the cups from the hot water and cool them on a rack or they will continue to cook while sitting in the hot water.

Indian Pudding Congolese

This tasty and economical dessert crosses oceans and generations with ease.

1 cup milk
1/2 cup yellow cornmeal
1 cup prepared coffee
1/2 cup molasses
2 tablespoons butter or margarine,
   room temperature

1/2 teaspoon salt
2 eggs, well beaten
1 teaspoon mixed apple pie spice
1/2 cup raisins
Sweetened Whipped Cream, page 122,
   or vanilla ice cream

Preheat oven to 300°F (150°C). Butter a 1-1/2 quart soufflé dish or deep casserole. In top of double boiler over medium heat, bring milk to a simmer. Stir in cornmeal. Place pan over, not in, simmering water. Cook, stirring often, until thickened and smooth. Add coffee and molasses. Blend and remove from heat. Add butter or margarine. Stir until melted. Add salt and eggs. Beat until thoroughly blended. Stir in apple pie spice and raisins. Pour into prepared soufflé dish or casserole. Bake in preheated oven 1-1/2 hours or until firm. Top with Sweetened Whipped Cream or vanilla ice cream. Makes 6 to 8 servings.

Kaiser Schmarren

The name may sound like nonsense but there's no nonsense about the taste!

1 cup prepared hot coffee
1 cup raisins
1 (9-inch) sponge cake

1/2 cup butter or margarine (1 stick), melted
1/2 pint dairy sour cream, chilled

Preheat oven to 425°F (220°C). In a medium bowl, pour coffee over raisins; set aside. Tear sponge cake into small pieces with a fork. Mix with raisins and coffee. Place in a 1-quart soufflé dish or casserole. Pour melted butter or margarine over surface. Bake in preheated oven 4 to 5 minutes. Serve hot. Top each serving with chilled sour cream. Makes 6 to 8 servings.

To prevent a film from forming on top of refrigerated puddings, place wax paper or plastic wrap directly on the surface of the warm pudding.

Holiday Mincemeat Pudding

The perfect steamed pudding for your busiest holidays!

1 tablespoon butter or margarine,
   room temperature
1 tablespoon granulated sugar
1-1/4 cups sifted all-purpose flour
1 teaspoon instant nonfat dry milk powder
2 teaspoons baking powder
2 tablespoons graham cracker crumbs
2 tablespoons more butter or margarine,
   room temperature

1/2 cup brown sugar, firmly packed
1 egg
1 cup prepared mincemeat
1/3 cup prepared coffee
1/2 cup chopped walnuts
Hard Sauce, see below

Hard Sauce:
3 tablespoons butter or margarine
3/4 cup sifted powdered sugar
3 tablespoons heated brandy or rum or
   1 teaspoon imitation brandy or rum
   flavoring plus 3 tablespoons milk

Coat a 1-pound coffee can with 1 tablespoon butter or margarine. Sprinkle with granulated sugar. Cover with plastic top; shake until sides and bottom are evenly coated with sugar. Sift together flour, dry milk powder and baking powder. Stir in graham cracker crumbs. In a large bowl, cream 2 tablespoons butter or margarine with brown sugar. Add egg. Beat until smooth. In a small bowl, combine mincemeat and coffee. Alternately add flour mixture and coffee-mincemeat mixture to creamed mixture, blending well after each addition. Stir in walnuts. Pour into prepared can. Cover can loosely with aluminum foil and secure with rubber band. Place on rack in a large heavy pot. Pour water into pot to bottom of rack. Cover pot. Steam for about 1-1/2 hours or until knife inserted in center of pudding comes out clean. If needed, add additional water to pot to maintain water level just below rack. Prepare Hard Sauce while pudding steams. To unmold pudding, turn can upside down on plate and open bottom of can with can opener; pudding will slide out onto plate. Slice and serve warm or at room temperature. Top with Hard Sauce. Makes 6 servings.

Hard Sauce:
In a small saucepan, melt butter or margarine. Remove from heat. Stir in powdered sugar and brandy or rum or brandy or rum flavoring plus milk. Beat until smooth. Refrigerate until ready to use.

Floating Island

A ring of meringue, lightly glazed with Caramel-Coffee Sauce, floats on delicate custard.

1 cup milk	3 tablespoons all-purpose flour
1 cup prepared coffee	1 teaspoon vanilla extract
5 egg yolks	Meringue, see below
1/2 cup sugar	Caramel-Coffee Sauce, see below

Meringue:

5 egg whites, room temperature	Dash salt
1/8 teaspoon cream of tartar	1/2 cup sugar

Caramel-Coffee Sauce:
1/2 cup sugar
1/2 cup prepared hot coffee

Place milk and coffee in a small saucepan over medium heat until bubbles appear around edge. In a medium saucepan, combine egg yolks, sugar and flour. Blend well. Slowly add hot milk-coffee mixture. Stir until blended. Stir over low heat until custard thickens enough to coat wooden spoon. Stir in vanilla extract. Pour into a serving bowl. Place a sheet of wax paper directly on top of custard. Refrigerate until chilled. Prepare Meringue. Remove wax paper from chilled custard. With a knife, loosen meringue from sides of mold. Invert to unmold onto custard. Refrigerate until chilled. Prepare Caramel-Coffee Sauce. Spoon over meringue just before serving.

Meringue:
Preheat oven to 350°F (175°C). Butter a 6-cup ring mold. In a medium bowl, beat egg whites with cream of tartar and salt until foamy. Add sugar 2 tablespoons at a time, beating well after each addition. Continue beating until stiff peaks form when beaters are slowly lifted from bowl. With a large spoon, press meringue lightly to remove air bubbles. Spoon into prepared mold. Place mold in a large baking pan. Pour hot water into pan to cover 3/4 of mold height. Bake in preheated oven 30 minutes or until knife inserted near center comes out clean.

Caramel-Coffee Sauce:
In a small skillet over medium heat, stir sugar until dissolved to a golden syrup. Pour in hot coffee. Syrup will harden; continue stirring over medium heat until hardened syrup dissolves in coffee. Cool slightly.

Don't overcook custards. A boiled custard is ready to be removed from the heat when it coats a wooden spoon. The custard may appear thin but it thickens as it cools.

Kentucky Puddin'

Down-home flavor in sweet potato pudding.

1-1/2 cups prepared coffee
3 medium sweet potatoes or yams
3 eggs, well beaten
2 cups sugar

1 teaspoon cinnamon
1/2 cup slivered toasted almonds
4 tablespoons butter or margarine
1/2 cup blended whiskey or rum, if desired

Preheat oven to 300°F (150°C). Butter a 2-quart casserole; set aside. Pour coffee in a large bowl. Peel and grate potatoes or yams into coffee. Stir in beaten eggs, sugar, cinnamon and almonds. Place in prepared casserole. Dot evenly with butter or margarine. Bake in preheated oven 1-1/2 to 2 hours or until potatoes are tender and pudding is firm. If desired, pour whiskey or rum over surface; let stand 5 to 10 minutes before serving. Makes 6 to 8 servings.

Brandy Snifter Pudding

Sparkling coffee cubes in creamy, brandy-flavored pudding.

1 envelope unflavored gelatin
1/2 cup cold water
1-1/4 cups boiling water
1/2 cup brown sugar, firmly packed
2 tablespoons instant coffee powder
1 (3-3/4-oz.) pkg. vanilla instant pudding
   and pie filling mix

1-1/2 cups milk
1/4 cup brandy or
   2 teaspoons imitation brandy flavoring
   plus 1/4 cup milk

In a medium bowl, sprinkle gelatin over cold water. Let stand 5 minutes to soften. Add boiling water; blend. Add brown sugar and instant coffee powder. Stir until dissolved. Pour into an 8-inch square baking pan. Refrigerate until firm, about 3 hours. Cut into cubes. Prepare vanilla pudding with 1-1/2 cups milk and brandy or brandy flavoring plus 1/4 cup milk according to package directions. Spoon half the pudding into 4 to 6 brandy snifters or parfait glasses. Add about 3/4 of the coffee gelatin cubes. Cover with remaining pudding. Top with remaining cubes. Makes 4 to 6 servings.

Frozen Desserts

Coffee has the magical touch for lifting the simplest frozen dessert out of the ordinary and into the spectacular.

The frozen desserts in this book include coffee specialties from individual Black & White Satins, a sure teenage favorite, to the frozen extravaganza, Cherry-Chocolate Cake.

All are easy to make, in fact so easy you can prepare several in an afternoon and store them in your freezer to be ready when you need them. It takes no longer to make and store the beautiful Bombe Brazilian, a half dozen Caffè Tortonis and the Ice Cream Pie topped with crushed peanut brittle than to make and frost a layer cake. Another easy and beautiful dessert to make ahead is Black Devil Parfaits, a luscious blend of marshmallows, coffee, bitter chocolate and coffee ice cream.

If you use store-bought ice cream, buy the best quality available. Look for a brand with all natural ingredients. Cheap ice cream is often loaded with fillers that will cause your dessert to melt too quickly and detract from its flavor.

Most frozen desserts benefit by standing at room temperature a few moments before serving. It's difficult to eat a hard-as-a-rock ice cream pie or parfait, so give your dessert a little time to come to eating consistency; 10 to 15 minutes is usually ample.

If your dessert is to be unmolded and presented on a serving platter, dip the mold briefly in fairly warm, not hot, water and invert onto the platter. Or invert the mold onto the platter and cover briefly with a towel wrung out in hot water. If the mold is not to be served within a few minutes, return it unmolded to the freezer.

Elegant & Easy

Meatballs Smitaine, page 25
Freshly Cooked Rice
Snow Peas With
Sliced Water Chestnuts
Raspberry Parfaits, page 76
California Cappucino, page 20

Caffè Tortoni

A touch of romantic Napoli.

1/3 cup slivered almonds	1/8 teaspoon salt
1 pint vanilla or coffee ice cream	2 tablespoons sugar
1 egg white	1/4 teaspoon almond extract
1 tablespoon instant coffee powder	

Spread slivered almonds on a baking sheet. Toast 10 to 12 inches under broiler heat until lightly browned, stirring and turning several times. Cool. With hands, crumble rather coarsely; set aside. Place ice cream in a large bowl. Mash slightly and let stand at room temperature until slightly softened. In a small bowl, combine egg white, instant coffee powder and salt. Beat until frothy. Gradually beat in sugar until soft peaks form when beaters are lifted from bowl. Stir in almond extract. Pour over softened ice cream. Beat with electric mixer on high speed until blended. Or with a large wooden spoon, fold together until blended. Pour into 6 fluted foil baking cups, half-cup baking cups or demitasse cups. Sprinkle with crumbled toasted almonds. Freeze until firm. If desired, wrap individually in foil and store in freezer until serving time. Makes 6 servings.

Spumone Delvino

Begin this special spumone from Rome's Delvino Restaurant 1 to 2 weeks ahead of time.

1 (4-oz.) jar maraschino cherries	1 pint chocolate ice cream
About 1/3 cup brandy	Vanilla cookie wafer crumbs, if desired
1 pint coffee ice cream, slightly softened	Sweetened Whipped Cream, page 122,
1 tablespoon instant coffee powder	if desired
1 pint vanilla ice cream	

Drain syrup from cherries. Pour brandy into jar over cherries, filling jar to brim. Cover. Refrigerate 1 to 2 weeks. Chill a 9" x 5" metal loaf pan in freezer. Spoon coffee ice cream into chilled pan and smooth to make an even layer. Sprinkle with instant coffee powder. Freeze. Place vanilla ice cream in a chilled bowl. Let stand at room temperature until slightly softened. Drain brandy from maraschino cherries; reserve brandy. Chop cherries and add to vanilla ice cream. Spoon and smooth over frozen coffee ice cream in loaf pan. Freeze. Place chocolate ice cream in a chilled bowl. Let stand at room temperature until slightly softened. Pour reserved brandy from cherries over chocolate ice cream. Blend well. Spoon over vanilla ice cream. Cover pan and seal with foil. Freeze. To serve, remove from freezer and let stand about 15 minutes. With a knife or spatula, loosen ice cream from sides of pan. Invert onto a serving platter. Dip a large towel in very hot water and wring out. Place over outside of mold. Mold will lift off easily. If desired, use a pastry tube to garnish with Sweetened Whipped Cream around base and top. Slice with a sharp knife dipped in very hot water. Makes 6 to 8 servings.

Raspberry Parfaits

Beautifully layered coffee ice cream, raspberry sherbet and coffee-chocolate syrup.

2 tablespoons instant coffee powder
2 tablespoons water
1-1/2 cups canned chocolate syrup (12-oz.)
1 qt. coffee ice cream

1 qt. raspberry sherbet
Sweetened Whipped Cream, page 122
8 to 10 very thin, square chocolate mints

Chill 8 to 10 parfait glasses or large wine glasses. Dissolve instant coffee powder in water. Stir into chocolate syrup. In chilled glasses, alternate generous layers of coffee ice cream and raspberry sherbet with thin layers of coffee-chocolate syrup. Freeze until serving time. Just before serving, top with Sweetened Whipped Cream and garnish with a chocolate mint. Makes 8 to 10 servings.

How To Make Raspberry Parfaits

1/Press a large spoonful of coffee ice cream into the bottom of a chilled parfait or wine glass. Top with a thin layer of coffee-chocolate syrup. Add a generous layer of raspberry sherbet. Top with another thin layer of syrup and a generous layer of ice cream. To make a neater parfait, place in freezer after adding each layer of syrup.

2/Freeze until ready to serve. Just before serving, top with whipped cream and garnish with a thin chocolate mint.

Bee Keeper's Sundaes

A honey of a dish!

3/4 cup slivered blanched almonds
1 cup honey
2 tablespoons instant coffee powder
1 qt. coffee or vanilla ice cream

Sweetened Whipped Cream, page 122,
  if desired
Toasted slivered almonds, if desired

Spread blanched almonds on a baking sheet or aluminum foil. Place in a 350°F (175°C) oven until golden brown. Cool. In a saucepan, combine honey and instant coffee powder. Cook over moderate heat, stirring occasionally, until coffee dissolves and mixture is heated. Stir in cooled toasted almonds. Cool slightly. Place a scoop of ice cream in each of 6 to 8 parfait glasses. Spoon about 1-1/2 tablespoons honey sauce over each. Cover with remaining ice cream and top with remaining honey sauce. If desired, garnish with Sweetened Whipped Cream and slivered almonds. Makes 6 to 8 servings.

Cappucino Parfaits

An exquisite blend of gourmet flavors.

1 tablespoon instant coffee powder
2 tablespoons hot water
1 (8-oz.) bottle butterscotch sauce
1 teaspoon grated orange peel
1/2 teaspoon cinnamon

1 qt. coffee ice cream
Sweetened Whipped Cream, page 122,
  if desired
More grated orange peel, if desired

Stir instant coffee powder into hot water. Place butterscotch sauce in a small bowl. Stir in coffee mixture. Add 1 teaspoon grated orange peel and cinnamon. Blend. Spoon alternate layers of coffee ice cream and sauce in 8 parfait glasses. Store in freezer until serving time. If desired, top with Sweetened Whipped Cream and sprinkle with grated orange peel. Makes 6 to 8 servings.

Lemon-Coffee Ice

Refreshing ending to a warm-weather dinner.

1/2 cup prepared cold coffee
1-1/2 pint lemon sherbet

2 tablespoons grenadine syrup

Place ingredients in blender container. Blend at low speed for 1 or 2 seconds. Spoon into 4 tall glasses. Makes 4 servings.

Plains Sundae Special

Ice cream with creamy smooth peanut butter and coffee sauce topped with crunchy peanuts.

1/2 cup light brown sugar, firmly packed	2 tablespoons butter or margarine
1 tablespoon corn syrup	1/2 cup smooth peanut butter
3/4 cup milk	1 qt. vanilla ice cream
2 tablespoons instant coffee powder	1 cup coarsely chopped peanuts

Chill 6 to 8 parfait glasses in freezer. In top of double boiler, combine brown sugar, corn syrup and milk. Stir over low heat until mixture comes to a boil. Lower heat and simmer about 15 minutes. Remove from heat. Add instant coffee powder; stir until dissolved. Add butter or margarine and peanut butter. Stir until melted. Keep warm over hot water. Place a scoop of ice cream in the bottom of chilled parfait glasses. Cover with a little warm sauce. Add another scoop of ice cream and more sauce. Sprinkle with chopped peanuts. Makes 6 to 8 servings.

Black & White Satins

Start with a spoon, then sip the last luscious bit with a straw.

4 small scoops chocolate ice cream	2 cups prepared hot coffee
4 small scoops vanilla ice cream	Whipped cream

Place 1 scoop each chocolate and vanilla ice cream in 4 tall glasses. Pour hot coffee equally over ice cream and top with whipped cream. Makes 4 servings.

Black Devil Parfaits

Easy to make and store—ready when you need them.

2 tablespoons instant coffee powder	2 (1-oz.) squares unsweetened chocolate
1 tablespoon hot water	1 qt. coffee ice cream
20 marshmallows	

Dissolve instant coffee powder in hot water. Combine marshmallows and chocolate in top of double boiler. Stir in coffee mixture. Cook over, not in, simmering water until marshmallows and chocolate melt and mixture is quite thick and smooth. Refrigerate until cool. Spoon alternate scoops of ice cream and chocolate-marshmallow mixture into 6 to 8 parfait glasses, ending with chocolate-marshmallow mixture. Cover with plastic wrap and store in freezer until serving time. Makes 6 to 8 servings.

Maple Velvets

Keep these lovely individual sweets in the freezer for unexpected dinner guests.

3/4 cup sugar
1/2 cup maple syrup
1 tablespoon instant coffee powder
4 egg yolks
1/4 cup prepared cold coffee

1 pint whipping cream
Shaved semisweet chocolate for garnish
Shredded dried coconut for garnish
Toasted slivered almonds for garnish
Ground walnuts for garnish

Combine sugar and maple syrup in a small saucepan. Bring to a boil. Cook to 234°F (112°C) on a candy thermometer or soft-ball stage. Remove syrup from heat. Add instant coffee powder. Stir until dissolved. In a medium bowl, beat egg yolks until thick and lemon-colored. Add syrup in a thin steady stream, beating constantly. Stir in cold coffee. Beat until very thick. Chill thoroughly. Beat cream until stiff. Fold into chilled custard. Pour into 8 fluted baking cups. Sprinkle 2 with shaved chocolate, 2 with shredded coconut, 2 with slivered almonds and 2 with ground walnuts. Freeze until firm. Wrap individually in aluminum foil. Store in freezer until serving time. Serve in foil cups. Makes 8 servings.

Banana Parfaits

Prepare the half chocolate and half coffee ice cream scoops ahead and store them in the freezer.

4 large ripe bananas, room temperature
1 teaspoon instant coffee powder
2 tablespoons dark rum
6 tablespoons whipping cream,
    room temperature

1 pint coffee ice cream
1 pint chocolate ice cream

Chill 6 dessert dishes or brandy snifters. Peel and thinly slice bananas. Place in a bowl. Sprinkle with instant coffee powder. Add rum and cream. Stir gently to coat evenly. Let stand at room temperature 10 to 15 minutes. Fill one side of an ice cream scoop with coffee ice cream and the other side with chocolate ice cream. Place in chilled dessert dishes or brandy snifters. Top with banana-cream mixture. Makes 6 servings.

When a recipe calls for slightly softened ice cream, chill a bowl in the freezer and place the frozen-solid ice cream in the chilled bowl. Let stand at room temperature until slightly softened.

How To Make
Brazilian Bombe

1/Press vanilla ice cream over bottom and sides of mold. Smooth a layer of raspberry sherbet over ice cream, forming a well in the center.

2/Fill center with whipped cream mixture. Cover the mold and wrap well with aluminum foil. Freeze several hours.

3/Unmold on serving platter just before serving. Sprinkle with instant coffee powder and cut into thick slices.

Brazilian Bombe

A bombe, pronounced bom, *is colorful circles of ice cream arranged in a round mold.*

1/2 cup brown sugar, firmly packed
2 tablespoons butter or margarine
1/4 cup prepared coffee
2 egg yolks, slightly beaten

1/2 pint whipping cream
1 pint vanilla ice cream, slightly softened
1/2 pint raspberry sherbet
1 tablespoon instant coffee powder for garnish

In a medium saucepan, combine brown sugar and butter or margarine. Stir over low heat until sugar melts. Add coffee and blend well. Remove from heat; cool slightly. Add beaten eggs. Beat until smooth. Return saucepan to low heat. Beat mixture until fluffy. Cool to room temperature. In a medium bowl, beat cream until stiff. Fold in cooled brown sugar mixture. Smooth vanilla ice cream over bottom and sides of a 2-quart bombe mold or round casserole. Line with a layer of raspberry sherbet, building up around the sides to form a well in the center. Fill center with whipped cream mixture. Cover and wrap mold in aluminum foil. Freeze several hours or overnight. Just before serving, unmold and sprinkle with instant coffee powder. Makes 10 to 12 servings.

New Year's Bombe

For any champagne celebration!

1/2 cup prepared coffee
1/4 cup sugar
1 envelope unflavored gelatin
1 pint whipping cream

1 cup crushed Pecan Brittle, page 135 or
   peanut brittle
1 qt. lemon sherbet

In a small saucepan, combine coffee, sugar and gelatin. Stir over low heat until sugar and gelatin dissolve. Remove from heat. Cool slightly. In a medium bowl, beat cream until stiff. Fold in gelatin mixture and crushed Pecan Brittle. Smooth lemon sherbet over bottom and sides of a 2-quart bombe mold or round casserole. Fill center with whipped cream mixture. Cover and wrap mold in aluminum foil. Freeze several hours or overnight. Unmold about 10 minutes before serving. To serve, slice into wedges. Makes about 8 servings.

To keep a frozen dessert at its peak of perfection, freeze until very firm, wrap in heavy aluminum foil, seal and return it to the freezer. This prevents loss of flavor and the formation of ice crystals.

Ice Cream Pie

Crushed pecan or peanut brittle tops this superb coffee pie.

1 envelope unflavored gelatin
1/4 cup sugar
1 cup prepared hot coffee
1 pint coffee ice cream
1 (9-inch) pie shell, baked and cooled

1 envelope whipped topping mix
1/2 cup prepared ice-cold coffee
1/2 teaspoon vanilla extract
1/4 cup crumbled Pecan Brittle, page 135
   or peanut brittle

Combine gelatin and sugar in a medium bowl. Add hot coffee. Stir until gelatin and sugar dissolve. Add ice cream by spoonfuls, stirring after each addition until melted and smooth. Pour into pie shell. Refrigerate until firm. Just before serving, chill a small bowl and beaters in freezer. In chilled bowl, combine whipped topping mix, ice-cold coffee and vanilla extract. Beat with electric mixer on high speed about 2 minutes until stiff peaks form when beaters are slowly lifted from bowl. Whip another 2 minutes until topping is light and fluffy. Spoon over pie. Sprinkle with crumbled Pecan-Brittle or peanut brittle. Makes one 9-inch pie.

Mousseline Parfaits

You can prepare the delicate custard sauce ahead and store it in the refrigerator up to a week.

2 egg yolks
1/3 cup sugar
2 teaspoons instant coffee powder
Pinch salt
2 tablespoons brandy or 1 teaspoon
   imitation brandy flavoring

1/2 pint whipping cream
1-1/2 qts. chocolate ice cream
Chopped walnuts for garnish

Combine egg yolks, sugar, instant coffee powder and salt in top of double boiler over, not in, simmering water. Beat until thickened to a custard-like sauce and about tripled in volume. Stir in brandy or brandy flavoring. Cool to room temperature. Refrigerate until ready to make parfaits. Beat cream until stiff. Fold in cooled custard. Refrigerate until chilled. Spoon alternate layers of ice cream and custard into parfait glasses. Top with chopped walnuts. Makes 8 to 10 servings.

Mocha-Bourbon Ice Cream

Jazz up the party with this New Orleans inspired treat.

3 (1-oz.) squares unsweetened chocolate
1-1/2 cups milk
1 cup light brown sugar, firmly packed
1/8 teaspoon salt

3 tablespoons instant coffee powder
1/2 cup bourbon
4 egg yolks
1 pint whipping cream

Combine chocolate, milk, brown sugar and salt in top of double boiler. Place over, not in, simmering water until chocolate melts. Add instant coffee powder and bourbon. Stir until smooth. In a small bowl, beat egg yolks until blended. Stir in a little hot chocolate mixture then stir egg-chocolate mixture into remaining hot chocolate mixture. Stir over hot water until mixture thickens and coats a wooden spoon. Cool. Stir in cream. Freeze in an ice cream maker following manufacturer's directions. Makes 2 quarts.

Poires Hélène

An impressive fruit and ice cream dessert.

1-1/2 cups water
1 cup sugar
1 vanilla bean or 1/2 teaspoon vanilla extract
6 ripe pears

1-1/2 cups Mint-Coffee Sauce, page 121
2 tablespoons instant coffee powder
6 scoops vanilla ice cream

In a large saucepan, combine water, sugar and vanilla bean. If using vanilla extract, reserve for later. Bring mixture to a boil over moderate heat. Lower heat and simmer about 10 minutes. Peel pears, cut in half and remove cores. Add to syrup and cook until soft enough to cut with a spoon. Remove from heat. If using vanilla extract, stir it into the syrup. Cool pears in syrup to room temperature. Refrigerate until chilled. Prepare Mint-Coffee Sauce. Stir in instant coffee powder. Keep at room temperature. Chill 6 dessert dishes. To serve, place 2 pear halves on each of 6 chilled dessert dishes. Top with vanilla syrup. Place a scoop of vanilla ice cream between pear halves. Serve Mint-Coffee Sauce separately. Makes 6 servings.

If you buy ice cream in gallon or half-gallon containers, use what you need and tightly wrap the remaining ice cream in its container in heavy aluminum foil and seal. Ice cream stored this way in the freezer will keep its original flavor and texture for several weeks.

The Ultimate Coffee Ice Cream

Everyone loves to make ice cream, especially if it's this good!

1/2 cup fine grind, dark-roast coffee
3-1/2 cups light cream
1 cup sugar
8 egg yolks

1/4 teaspoon salt
1/2 cup Alice Hasting's Coffee Liqueur,
    page 156, or other coffee liqueur
Candy coffee beans, if desired

Place ground coffee in a medium bowl. In a small saucepan, heat cream to scalding or just below boiling, about 180°F (80°C). Pour over ground coffee. Cover and let stand about 30 minutes. Line a fine sieve with a double thickness of cheesecloth. Strain coffee-cream mixture through cheesecloth into a large saucepan. Add sugar. Heat to scalding; do not boil. In a medium bowl, beat egg yolks with salt until very pale and thick. Slowly add the scalded mixture, beating constantly. Pour into a medium saucepan. Stir over medium heat until mixture thickens and coats a wooden spoon. Stir in liqueur. Place saucepan in a large bowl of ice water. Stir until cooled. If desired, cover surface of custard with wax paper and place in refrigerator until ready to freeze. Freeze in an ice cream maker following manufacturer's instructions. Serve in parfait glasses. If desired, garnish with candy coffee beans. Makes about 1-1/2 quarts.

Jamaican Ice Cream

Flavor from the romantic Caribbean.

2 cups milk
1/2 cup sugar
2 tablespoons all-purpose flour
2 eggs, well beaten
1/2 teaspoon salt

1 envelope unflavored gelatin
1/4 cup cold water
3 tablespoons instant coffee powder
1/4 cup dark Jamaican rum
1 pint whipping cream

Place milk in a large saucepan over low heat until small bubbles appear around edge and milk is steaming hot. Combine sugar and flour in a small bowl. Stir in about 1/2 cup hot milk then stir milk-flour mixture into remaining hot milk. Stir over low heat until smooth. Stir about 1/4 cup milk-flour mixture into beaten eggs then stir egg-milk mixture into remaining milk-flour mixture. Add salt. Stir over low heat to a smooth thick custard. Remove from heat. Sprinkle gelatin over cold water. Let stand 5 minutes to soften. Stir into hot custard. Stir in instant coffee powder and rum. Beat until custard has cooled to room temperature. In a medium bowl, beat cream until stiff. Fold in custard mixture. Freeze in an ice cream maker following manufacturer's instructions. Makes 2 quarts.

Cherry-Chocolate Cake

You'll need your largest dessert plates to serve this unique cake.

1 qt. coffee ice cream, slightly softened
1 qt. cherry ice cream, slightly softened
3 (9-inch) round chocolate cake layers,
    made from 1 (18.5-oz.) pkg. chocolate
    cake mix according to pkg. directions
    using coffee for required liquid

6 tablespoons prepared cold coffee
1 pint whipping cream
1/2 cup powdered sugar
2 tablespoons rum or 1 teaspoon
    rum flavoring
Chocolate Curls for Garnish, see below

Chocolate Curls:
1 (1-oz.) square semisweet chocolate

Line four 9-inch, round cake pans with plastic wrap. Quickly spread half the coffee ice cream evenly in 1 pan and half in another pan. Cover and wrap pans in aluminum foil. Freeze. Repeat with cherry ice cream in remaining 2 pans. Chill a serving plate in freezer. Place 1 chocolate cake layer on chilled plate. Sprinkle with 2 tablespoons coffee. Unwrap 1 pan with cherry ice cream and invert on cake. Lift off pan and peel off plastic wrap. Repeat with 1 pan coffee ice cream. Place second chocolate cake layer on top of ice cream. Sprinkle with 2 tablespoons coffee. Top with remaining ice cream layers. Place last cake layer on top and sprinkle with remaining 2 tablespoons coffee. Place cake in freezer. Whip cream until stiff. Fold in powdered sugar and rum or rum flavoring. Frost top and sides of cake. Place in freezer until frosting is very firm. Just before serving, sprinkle top of cake with Chocolate Curls. Makes one 3-layer, 9-inch, round cake.

Chocolate Curls:
Slightly soften square of chocolate on aluminum foil in a warm oven. With a small sharp knife or vegetable parer, shave thin curls of chocolate onto top of cake.

Almond Custards

Make these up during the week and they'll be ready for the weekend.

2 eggs
1/2 cup sugar
1/8 teaspoon salt
2 tablespoons instant coffee powder

1/2 pint whipping cream
1/2 teaspoon almond extract
1/2 cup chopped toasted almonds
Toasted slivered almonds, if desired

Place eggs, sugar and salt in a small bowl. Place bowl in a pan of hot water. Beat with electric mixer or rotary beater until very light and fluffy. Add instant coffee powder. Continue to beat until tripled in volume. Remove bowl from hot water. In a large bowl, beat cream until stiff. Fold about 2 tablespoons whipped cream into egg-coffee mixture. Fold egg-coffee mixture into whipped cream. Fold in almond extract and chopped almonds. Spoon into 6 parfait glasses or eight 4-ounce paper cupcake cups. If desired, sprinkle slivered almonds over each serving. Freeze. Cover each dessert with aluminum foil. Store in freezer until serving time. Makes 6 to 8 servings.

Cakes

Welcome to my priceless collection of cakes made with coffee. Some became famous—almost legendary—through the years. Others are adaptations of recently popular cakes and store-bought mixes.

What type of cake do you prefer? Dark rich mocha? Light coffee sponge? You'll find your favorite here. To give your baking variety, each cake has a different and delicious filling, frosting, glaze or topping; each is made doubly delicious with coffee's magical flavor and every recipe has easy-to-follow directions for perfect results.

Making cakes is easy. The basic preparation is always essentially the same.
- Make sure you have the proper size and type of pan. A too large, too deep or too small pan can spoil the most carefully made cake.
- Coat the pan completely with oil or butter as directed. A missed spot means a stuck cake and that's a disappointment.
- Have all your ingredients at room temperature for easy mixing and blending.
- Assemble all your ingredients before starting your cake. Stopping to look for a flavoring or the baking powder is not the road to successful cake making.

You probably already have the proper tools on hand. They include a large mixing bowl and 1 or 2 smaller ones for whipping eggs or cream or coating nuts or fruit with flour. A big wooden mixing spoon and a wire whisk are indispensable. Although any cake in this book can be made without an electric mixer, there is no doubt this appliance saves time and effort. In most cases a simple hand mixer will do nicely. You'll also need a wooden chopping board and a sharp knife or cleaver for chopping nuts and fruits, measuring cups and spoons and 1 or 2 cake racks. A cake not cooled on a rack can become soggy or—even worse—break when you attempt to transfer it to a serving platter.

If you agree with me that there is no better treat than a piece of homemade cake and a steaming cup of freshly made coffee, turn the pages of this section and enjoy!

Come For Dessert & Coffee

Glazed Bundt Cake

Made fast from a mix.

1 tablespoon butter or margarine,
   room temperature
4 to 5 tablespoons ground walnuts
1 (18.5-oz.) pkg. yellow cake mix
1 (3-3/4-oz.) pkg. instant vanilla pudding
   and pie filling

1/2 cup vegetable oil
1 cup prepared coffee
4 eggs
Coffee-Sugar Glaze, see below
Ground walnuts for garnish

Coffee-Sugar Glaze:
1 cup powdered sugar
1-1/2 tablespoons prepared coffee

Preheat oven to 325°F (165°C). Coat a 10-inch bundt pan with 1 tablespoon butter or margarine. Sprinkle with 4 to 5 tablespoons ground walnuts. Rotate pan to distribute nuts evenly; set pan aside. In a medium bowl, blend cake mix with pudding mix. Add oil, coffee and eggs. Beat with electric mixer on medium speed 2 minutes. Pour into prepared pan. Bake in preheated oven 50 to 55 minutes or until top springs back when lightly touched with fingertips. Cool cake in pan on rack about 30 minutes. Turn out onto rack. Cool completely. Prepare Coffee-Sugar Glaze. Spoon over top of cake, letting it run down sides. Sprinkle with ground walnuts. Makes one 10-inch bundt cake.

Coffee-Sugar Glaze:
In a small bowl, combine sugar and coffee. Blend well.

Denver City Pudding Cake

Cake on top—pudding on the bottom.

3/4 cup all-purpose flour
3 teaspoons baking powder
1/8 teaspoon salt
3/4 cup sugar
1/4 cup fine dry breadcrumbs
3 tablespoons butter or margarine
3 tablespoons cocoa powder
1 egg, slightly beaten

1/3 cup milk, room temperature
1/2 teaspoon vanilla extract
3/4 cup brown sugar, firmly packed
1/4 cup more fine dry breadcrumbs
1/4 cup more cocoa powder
1-1/2 cup prepared strong black coffee,
   room temperature
Vanilla ice cream or chilled whipped cream

Preheat oven to 350°F (175°C). Generously butter a 9-inch square baking pan; set aside. Sift together flour, baking powder and salt into a medium bowl. Stir in sugar and 1/4 cup breadcrumbs. In a small saucepan melt butter or margarine. Stir in 3 tablespoons cocoa powder; continue stirring until smooth. Remove from heat. Cool slightly. Stir in egg. Add milk. Stir until smooth. Stir in vanilla extract. Stir cocoa-milk mixture into flour mixture. Blend well. Pour into prepared pan. Sift brown sugar over surface, sprinkle with 1/4 cup breadcrumbs and 1/4 cup cocoa powder. Do not stir or mix. Carefully pour coffee over all. Again, do not stir or mix. Bake in preheated oven 40 to 45 minutes or until top is crusty. Do not chill. Serve warm or at room temperature with vanilla ice cream or chilled whipped cream. Makes 6 to 8 servings.

Mountain Cake

A high and light coffee-flavored sponge cake with white-as-snow frosting.

1-3/4 cups cake flour
1 teaspoon baking powder
1/4 cup fine dry breadcrumbs

4 eggs, room temperature
1-1/2 cups sugar
1 cup prepared hot coffee

Top-of-the-Peak Frosting:
2 egg whites
3/4 cup sugar
1/3 cup corn syrup
2 tablespoons water

1/4 teaspoon cream of tartar
1/4 teaspoon salt
4 marshmallows
1/2 teaspoon almond extract

Preheat oven to 350°F (175°C). Sift together flour and baking powder. Add breadcrumbs. Mix well. In a large bowl, beat eggs and sugar with electric mixer on high speed about 5 minutes until very light and fluffy. Add flour mixture alternately with coffee. Fold and stir only until blended. Pour into an ungreased 9-inch tube pan. Bake in preheated oven 35 to 40 minutes or until top springs back when lightly touched with fingertips. Invert cake on rack and cool completely before removing from pan. Prepare Top-of-the-Peak Frosting. Loosen cake from sides of pan with a knife. Turn out onto rack. Frost top and sides of cake. Makes one 9-inch tube cake.

Top-of-the-Peak Frosting:
Place egg whites, sugar, corn syrup, water, cream of tartar and salt in top of double boiler over, not in, simmering water. Beat with electric mixer on high speed until light and fluffy. Add marshmallows. Stir until marshmallows melt. Beat until frosting is very thick and holds firm peaks when beaters are slowly lifted from pan. Stir in almond extract.

Almond Torte

Inspired by the famous cakes of Vienna.

9 eggs
1 cup pitted dates
1/2 cup slivered almonds
1/2 cup prepared cold coffee
1-3/4 cups sugar

1 teaspoon cinnamon
1 teaspoon ground allspice
1-1/2 cups fine graham cracker crumbs
1/2 teaspoon baking powder
Whipped cream or dairy sour cream

Preheat oven to 350°F (175°C). Lightly oil a 9-inch springform pan. Dust with flour and rotate pan to coat evenly. Shake out excess flour; set pan aside. Separate 7 of the eggs. Place egg whites in a small bowl, egg yolks in a medium bowl. Add the remaining 2 whole eggs to yolks. Set aside to come to room temperature. Combine dates, almonds and coffee in blender container. Blend to puree. Beat egg yolks and whole eggs with sugar until thickened and pale. Fold in date-almond puree. In a small bowl, thoroughly mix cinnamon, allspice, graham cracker crumbs and baking powder. Fold into batter. Beat egg whites until very stiff. Fold into batter. Pour into prepared pan. Bake 50 to 60 minutes. Invert onto rack; let cool 5 to 10 minutes before removing cake from pan. Serve with whipped cream or sour cream. Makes one 9-inch cake.

Koffee Klatch Cake

An easy mix!

1 cup prepared coffee, room temperature	1/4 cup cocoa powder
3/4 cup honey	1/2 teaspoon salt
1/2 cup corn or safflower oil	1/4 teaspoon ground allspice
1 teaspoon vanilla extract	1/4 teaspoon ground cloves
1 tablespoon vinegar	1 teaspoon baking soda
1-1/2 cups all-purpose flour	

Preheat oven to 300°F (150°C). Oil an 8-inch square baking pan; set aside. In a small bowl, combine coffee, honey, oil, vanilla extract and vinegar. Stir to blend well. Sift remaining ingredients into medium bowl. Add coffee-honey mixture. Stir to blend. Pour into prepared pan. Bake in preheated oven 1 hour to 1 hour and 15 minutes or until top springs back when lightly touched with fingertips. Cool in pan on rack 5 minutes. Cut into squares and serve warm from the pan. Makes one 8-inch square cake.

Mary Anna's Rum Cake

An extra-sweet glaze for an extraordinary cake.

3-1/2 cups cake flour	1 cup butter or margarine (2 sticks), room temperature
4 tablespoons instant nonfat dry milk powder	2 cups sugar
1 tablespoon baking powder	3 eggs
1/4 teaspoon salt	1 cup prepared coffee, room temperature

Coffee-Rum Glaze:

1 cup light brown sugar, firmly packed	1 cup prepared coffee
1 cup granulated sugar	2 tablespoons light rum or
2 tablespoons butter or margarine, room temperature	1/2 teaspoon imitation rum flavoring

Preheat oven to 325°F (165°C). Butter a 9-inch tube pan or kugelhopf pan. Dust with flour and rotate pan to coat evenly. Shake out excess flour; set pan aside. Sift together flour, dry milk powder, baking powder and salt. In a large bowl, cream butter or margarine with sugar until very light and fluffy. Add eggs 1 at a time, beating well after each addition. Add flour mixture alternately with coffee, beginning and ending with flour mixture. Pour into prepared pan. Bake in preheated oven 1 hour and 20 to 30 minutes or until cake shrinks from sides of pan slightly and top springs back when lightly touched. Prepare Coffee-Rum Glaze. Place cake in pan on rack. Slowly pour half of glaze over top of cake. Let stand 30 minutes. Invert onto cake plate. Remove pan and pour on remaining glaze. Makes one 9-inch tube cake.

Coffee-Rum Glaze:
In a medium saucepan, combine sugars, butter or margarine and coffee. Bring to a boil over medium heat, stirring constantly. Reduce heat and simmer 3 to 4 minutes. Stir in rum or rum flavoring.

Java Spice Cake

Moist, rich, subtly flavored spice cake is iced to perfection with creamy smooth Coffee Frosting.

2 cups prepared hot strong coffee
1 cup finely chopped pitted prunes
3/4 cup raisins
1 cup finely chopped pecans
2-3/4 cups cake flour
1 tablespoon baking powder
1/2 teaspoon baking soda
1/2 teaspoon ground allspice

1/2 teaspoon finely ground black pepper
6 tablespoons butter or margarine,
    room temperature
1-1/2 cups sugar
3 eggs
Coffee Frosting, see below
Pecan halves for garnish

Coffee Frosting:

1/2 cup butter or margarine (1 stick),
    room temperature
2 (3-oz.) pkgs. cream cheese,
    room temperature
3 tablespoons instant coffee powder,
    dissolved in 6 tablespoons prepared
    hot coffee

7 to 8 cups sifted powdered sugar
3 to 4 drops Angostura bitters
More powdered sugar, if needed

Preheat oven to 350°F (175°C). Butter three 9-inch, round, layer cake pans. Dust with flour and rotate pans to coat evenly. Shake out excess flour; set pans aside. In a small bowl, pour hot coffee over prunes and raisins. In another small bowl, mix pecans with 1/4 cup flour. Sift together remaining flour, baking powder, baking soda, allspice and pepper. In a large bowl, cream butter or margarine with sugar. Add eggs. Beat until light and fluffy. Add flour mixture alternately with prune-coffee mixture, stirring well after each addition. Fold in flour-coated pecans. Pour into prepared pans. Bake in preheated oven 30 to 40 minutes or until top springs back when lightly touched with fingertips. Turn out onto rack. Cool completely. Prepare Coffee Frosting. Put layers together with about half the frosting. Cover sides and top with remaining frosting. Garnish with pecan halves. Makes one 3-layer, 9-inch, round cake.

Coffee Frosting:
Cream butter or margarine and cream cheese until smooth. Add dissolved coffee. Beat until blended. Add powdered sugar. Continue to beat until light and fluffy. Stir in bitters. If needed, add more powdered sugar to bring to spreading consistency.

Honey Snack Cake

While the youngsters devour it with milk, enjoy your smuggled piece with a cup of coffee.

1 tablespoon all-purpose flour
1/2 cup chopped pecans
2 cups more all-purpose flour
1 teaspoon baking powder
1/2 teaspoon baking soda
1/4 teaspoon salt
2 teaspoons apple pie spice

1/2 cup butter or margarine (1 stick),
   room temperature
1/2 cup sugar
1/2 cup honey
3 eggs
1/2 cup prepared coffee
Powdered sugar

Preheat oven to 350°F (175°C). Butter a 9-inch square baking pan; set aside. Stir 1 tablespoon flour into chopped pecans; set aside. Sift together 2 cups flour, baking powder, baking soda, salt and apple pie spice. In a medium bowl, cream butter or margarine with sugar until light and fluffy. Beat in honey. Add eggs. Beat until light and smooth. Add flour mixture alternately with coffee, stirring well after each addition. Fold in pecan-flour mixture. Pour into prepared pan. Bake in preheated oven 35 to 40 minutes or until top springs back when lightly touched with fingertips. Cool in pan on rack 5 minutes. Turn out onto rack. Cool completely. Dust with powdered sugar. Cut into squares. Makes one 9-inch square cake.

Easy Pound Cake

Made from a mix but coffee and Apricot Filling make a delicious difference.

1/2 cup butter or margarine (1 stick),
   very soft
1 (1-lb.) pkg. pound cake mix
4 eggs

1/2 cup prepared coffee
1 teaspoon instant coffee powder
Apricot Filling, see below

Apricot Filling:
1 (6-oz.) pkg. dried apricots
Water
1 (8-oz.) pkg. cream cheese,
   room temperature

1 cup powdered sugar
2 teaspoons instant coffee powder

Preheat oven to 300°F (150°C). Butter a 9" x 5" loaf pan. Sprinkle with sugar and rotate pan to coat evenly. Shake out excess sugar; set pan aside. In a large bowl, combine softened butter or margarine with pound cake mix. Blend well. Add eggs 1 at a time, beating well after each addition. Add coffee and instant coffee powder. Blend well. Pour into prepared pan. Bake in preheated oven 1 hour and 30 minutes. Prepare Apricot Filling. Remove cake from pan at once and cool on a rack. Cut in half horizontally and spread bottom layer with half of Apricot Filling. Replace top half of cake. Spread with remaining filling. Chill or freeze before serving. Makes 1 loaf cake.

Apricot Filling:
Place apricots in a medium saucepan. Add water to cover. Cook over low heat until just tender. Drain. Chop apricots to a pulp. Combine with remaining ingredients in a large bowl. Beat well.

Gingerbread

Molasses, ginger and coffee make a gingerbread lover's dream.

1 cup prepared hot coffee
1 cup raisins
2 cups sifted all-purpose flour
2 teaspoons baking soda
1/2 teaspoon salt
1 teaspoon cinnamon
1 teaspoon ginger
1/2 teaspoon nutmeg

1/4 teaspoon ground cloves
1/2 cup butter or margarine (1 stick),
   room temperature
1/2 cup sugar
1 cup molasses
2 eggs
Confectioner's Citrus Glaze, see below

Confectioner's Citrus Glaze:
1 cup powdered sugar
1 to 2 tablespoons orange or lemon juice

Preheat oven to 350°F (175°C). Butter a 12" x 9" or 14" x 9" baking pan. Dust with flour and rotate pan to coat evenly. Shake out excess flour; set pan aside. Pour hot coffee over raisins. Cool to room temperature. Sift together flour, baking soda, salt, cinnamon, ginger, nutmeg and cloves. In a medium bowl, cream butter or margarine with sugar. Add molasses and eggs. Beat until thickened and pale. Stir in coffee-raisin mixture. Add flour mixture all at once and stir until thoroughly blended. Pour into prepared pan. Bake in preheated oven 40 to 45 minutes or until cake shrinks from side of pan and a wooden pick inserted in center comes out clean. Prepare Confectioner's Citrus Glaze. Cool cake in pan on rack. Cover warm cake with glaze. Cut into squares. Makes one 12" x 9" or 14" x 9" cake.

Confectioner's Citrus Glaze:
Mix powdered sugar with enough juice to bring to spreading consistency.

If you are using a recipe that calls for egg whites only, the yolks will stay fresh for several days if you place them in a small bowl and cover them gently with cold water. Cover the bowl with plastic wrap and store in the refrigerator until you can use the yolks in another recipe.

Dobos Torte

Golden cake layers with sweet syrup and chocolate icing.

3/4 cup butter or margarine
8 large eggs
1-1/3 cups sugar
1 teaspoon vanilla extract

1-1/3 cups cake flour, sifted
Coffee Syrup, see below
French Pastry Chef's Icing, see below
Walnut halves for garnish

Coffee Syrup:
1-1/2 cups prepared coffee
1 cup sugar

1/2 cup currant jelly

French Pastry Chef's Icing:
1/2 pint whipping cream
1 tablespoon instant coffee powder

2 (3-oz.) Swiss bittersweet chocolate bars

Preheat oven to 350°F (175°C). Butter three 9-inch layer cake pans. Dust with flour and rotate pans to coat evenly. Shake out excess flour; set pans aside. In a small saucepan, melt butter or margarine. Cool; set aside. Separate egg whites into a large bowl and yolks into a medium bowl. Beat whites until soft peaks form when beaters are slowly lifted from bowl. Add sugar 1/3 cup at a time. Continue beating until very stiff. Beat egg yolks with vanilla extract to a very light consistency and pale color. Stir in about 2 tablespoons beaten egg whites, then gently fold egg yolk mixture into remaining egg whites. Fold in flour about 1/3 cup at a time. Slowly fold in cooled melted butter or margarine. Spoon equally into prepared pans. Bake in preheated oven 20 to 25 minutes or until top springs back when lightly touched with fingertips. Turn out onto racks. Cool completely. Cut each cake into 2 layers to make a total of 6 cake layers. Prepare Coffee Syrup and French Pastry Chef's Icing. Place 1 cake layer on a cake plate. Pour 2 to 3 tablespoons Coffee Syrup over surface. Cover with a thin layer of icing. Repeat with remaining cake layers. Pour remaining icing over top of last layer and quickly spread on sides of cake. Decorate top with a ring of walnut halves. Makes one 6-layer, 9-inch, round cake.

Coffee Syrup:
Combine ingredients in a small saucepan. Stir over low heat until sugar and jelly dissolve. Cool to room temperature.

French Pastry Chef's Icing:
Combine ingredients in top of double boiler. Place over, not in, simmering water until chocolate melts and instant coffee powder dissolves. Stir until smooth. Keep warm over hot water until ready to use.

How To Make
Dobos Torte

1/Cut each cooled cake into 2 layers, making a total of 6 layers.

2/Pour about 1/3 cup Coffee Syrup over top of 1 cake layer.

3/Cover syrup with 2 to 3 tablespoons of icing and top with second cake layer. Repeat with remaining cake layers, syrup and icing. Spread remaining icing over the top and sides of torte. Garnish with walnut halves.

Black Forest Layer Cake

For the traditional afternoon coffee hour.

2-1/4 cups cake flour
2 tablespoons cocoa powder
2 tablespoons instant coffee powder
1 tablespoon vinegar
1 cup milk
1/2 cup butter or margarine (1 stick),
   room temperature
1/2 cup granulated sugar

1/2 cup light brown sugar, firmly packed
2 eggs
1 tablespoon Angostura bitters
1 teaspoon baking soda
1 tablespoon more vinegar
Cherry-Lemon Filling, see below
Wilhelm's Frosting, see page 99

Cherry-Lemon Filling:
1/3 cup sugar
1-1/2 tablespoons all-purpose flour
1-1/2 tablespoons cornstarch
1/8 teaspoon salt
1 cup milk

1 egg, well beaten
1/2 cup chopped maraschino cherries
1 teaspoon vanilla extract
1/2 teaspoon lemon extract

Preheat oven to 350°F (175°C). Oil two 9-inch layer cake pans and line bottoms of pans with wax paper. Coat wax paper with oil. Sift together flour, cocoa powder and instant coffee powder. Stir 1 tablespoon vinegar into milk. Cream butter or margarine with granulated and brown sugars. Add eggs and beat well. Add flour mixture alternately with milk-vinegar mixture, blending well after each addition. Stir in bitters. Dissolve baking soda in 1 tablespoon vinegar. Stir, do not beat, dissolved baking soda mixture into batter. Pour into prepared pans. Bake in preheated oven 25 to 30 minutes or until top of cake springs back when lightly touched with fingertips. Cool in pans on racks 5 minutes. Invert onto racks; remove pans. Cool slightly. Remove wax paper. Cool completely before putting together with Cherry-Lemon Filling and Wilhelm's Frosting. Makes one 2-layer, 9-inch, cake.

Cherry-Lemon Filling:
In top of double boiler, combine sugar, flour, cornstarch and salt. Stir to blend. Add milk and egg. Beat with electric mixer on medium speed until smooth and blended. Stir over, not in, simmering water until very thick and smooth. Remove pan from water. Fold in cherries and vanilla and lemon extracts. Place plastic wrap directly on surface of mixture. Cool. Refrigerate until thick.

Butter cream frostings may appear too thin to spread on the cake. To be safe, refrigerate the frosting at least 30 minutes before you decide to add more powdered sugar. As the frosting chills, it will harden to spreading consistency.

Wilhelm's Frosting

Every cake you make should get this kind of special treatment!

2 tablespoons instant coffee powder
2 tablespoons hot water
2 tablespoons kirsch liqueur or
   1/2 teaspoon lemon extract plus
   water to make 2 tablespoons

1/2 cup butter or margarine (1 stick),
   room temperature
1 (3-oz.) pkg. cream cheese,
   room temperature
3 cups powdered sugar

In a small bowl, combine instant coffee powder and hot water. Stir until coffee powder dissolves. Stir in liqueur or lemon extract mixture. Add butter or margarine and cream cheese. Beat until blended. Add powdered sugar a little at a time, beating until smooth and creamy. Chill slightly to bring to spreading consistency. Makes enough to frost one 9-inch, round layer cake.

Arabian Chocolate Cake

Chocolate spice cake with a cinnamon-cream filling.

1 tablespoon butter or margarine, softened
2 tablespoons fine dry breadcrumbs
1-3/4 cups flour
2 teaspoons baking powder
1 teaspoon cinnamon
1/4 teaspoon ground cloves
4 (1-oz.) squares unsweetened chocolate
4 tablespoons instant coffee powder
1/2 cup water

1/2 cup butter or margarine (1 stick),
   room temperature
1 cup granulated sugar
2 eggs
1/2 cup milk
1 teaspoon vanilla extract
Cinnamon-Cream Filling, see below
Powdered sugar

Cinnamon-Cream Filling:
1/2 pint whipping cream
2 tablespoons granulated sugar

1 tablespoon instant coffee powder
1/4 teaspoon cinnamon

Preheat oven to 350°F (175°C). Coat two 8-inch layer pans with 1 tablespoon butter or margarine. Sprinkle each with 1 tablespoon breadcrumbs; set pans aside. Sift together flour, baking powder, cinnamon and cloves. In top of double boiler over, not in, simmering water, melt chocolate with coffee and water. Remove from heat and stir to blend. In a large bowl, cream 1/2 cup butter or margarine with sugar. Add eggs. Beat until light and fluffy. Stir in coffee-chocolate mixture. Add flour mixture alternately with milk. Stir in vanilla extract. Spoon into prepared pans. Bake in preheated oven 25 minutes or until tops spring back when lightly touched with fingertips. Turn out onto racks. Cool. Prepare Cinnamon-Cream Filling. Put layers together with filling. Sprinkle top of cake with powdered sugar. Refrigerate until serving time. Makes one 2-layer, 8-inch, round cake.

Cinnamon-Cream Filling:
In a small bowl, whip cream until quite thick but not stiff. Combine sugar, instant coffee powder and cinnamon. Add gradually to cream. Whip until stiff.

Crumb Torte

A heavenly cake!

5 large eggs
1 cup sugar
2 cups graham cracker crumbs
   (22 crackers)

1 teaspoon baking powder
1 teaspoon vanilla extract
2 tablespoons instant coffee powder

Sugar-Cream Filling:
1/2 pint whipping cream
1/4 cup powdered sugar

Hungarian Mocha Icing:
2 (1-oz.) squares unsweetened chocolate
1/2 cup powdered sugar
1 tablespoon instant coffee powder
1 tablespoon water

1 egg, slightly beaten
3 tablespoons butter or margarine,
   room temperature

Preheat oven to 350°F (175°C). Generously butter two 9-inch layer cake pans. Dust with flour and rotate pans to coat evenly. Shake out excess flour; set pans aside. Separate egg whites into a medium bowl and egg yolks into a large bowl. Beat egg whites until stiff. Gradually beat in 1/4 cup of the sugar. In a large bowl, beat egg yolks until thickened and lemon-colored. Beat in remaining sugar. Add graham cracker crumbs, baking powder, vanilla extract and instant coffee powder. Fold in beaten egg whites. Spoon into prepared pans. Bake in preheated oven 20 to 25 minutes. Cool in pans on racks 5 to 10 minutes. Gently run a knife around cake edges, lifting slightly to loosen. Invert onto racks, remove pans and cool completely. Prepare Sugar-Cream Filling and Hungarian Mocha Icing. Put layers together with filling. Frost top generously with icing, letting it run down sides of cake. Makes one 2-layer, 9-inch, round cake.

Sugar-Cream Filling:
In a small bowl, beat cream until stiff. Fold in powdered sugar.

Hungarian Mocha Icing:
Melt chocolate in top of double boiler over, not in, simmering water. Stir in powdered sugar, instant coffee powder and water. Add egg. Stir over low heat 1 to 2 minutes. Remove from heat. Add butter or margarine. Beat until thickened and smooth.

If a freshly baked cake sticks to the pan, cool it in the pan on a rack 5 to 10 minutes. Then gently run a knife around the edge of the cake, lifting slightly to loosen the cake from the pan. Invert on the rack and remove pan to cool completely.

Easy-Mix Cake

Use leftover breakfast coffee to make this mixed-in-the-pan cake.

1 (15-oz.) pkg. applesauce-raisin cake mix
1 cup prepared coffee

Preheat oven to 350°F (175°C). Follow package directions substituting coffee for 1 cup required liquid. Bake in preheated oven 33 to 38 minutes. Cool in pan on rack 10 minutes. Makes one 8-inch square or 9-inch, round cake.

Fruit-Filled Loaf Cake

Convenient frozen pound cake with a fabulous filling.

1/2 cup prepared hot coffee
3/4 cup finely chopped mixed dried fruit
1/3 cup sugar
1-1/2 tablespoons cornstarch
1/2 cup more prepared coffee

2 tablespoons rum or brandy, or
  1 teaspoon imitation rum or
  brandy flavoring
Chocolate Cream Frosting, see below
1 (10-oz.) frozen pound cake

Chocolate Cream Frosting:
2 tablespoons prepared coffee
1 (1-oz.) square unsweetened chocolate
1 (8-oz.) pkg. cream cheese,
  room temperature

1-1/2 cups powdered sugar
More powdered sugar, if needed

Pour 1/2 cup hot coffee over chopped dried fruit in a small bowl. Let stand about 1 hour until all coffee is absorbed. In a medium saucepan, combine sugar, cornstarch, 1/2 cup coffee and rum, brandy or rum or brandy flavoring. Stir over medium heat until sugar dissolves and mixture thickens. Fold in dried fruit mixture. Cool until filling reaches room temperature and is very thick. Prepare Chocolate Cream Frosting. Cut cake into 3 horizontal slices. Spread first layer with fruit filling. Replace second layer; spread with fruit filling. Top with third layer. Frost top and sides with Chocolate Cream Frosting. Refrigerate or freeze until frosting is firm. If desired, wrap and store frozen cake in freezer. Makes one 3-layer loaf cake.

Chocolate Cream Frosting:
Place coffee and chocolate in top of double boiler over, not in, simmering water until chocolate melts. Stir to blend. Cool to room temperature. In a medium bowl, beat cream cheese until light and fluffy. Fold in chocolate mixture. Beat until smooth. Add powdered sugar. Blend well. Refrigerate until stiff enough to spread on cake. If needed, add more powdered sugar to bring to spreading consistency.

Mincemeat Squares

Enjoy holiday flavors all year 'round.

4 tablespoons instant coffee powder
1/4 cup hot water
2-1/2 cups all-purpose flour
1/2 teaspoon salt
1 teaspoon baking soda
1/2 cup butter or margarine (1 stick),
   room temperature

3/4 cup molasses
2 eggs
1 cup canned applesauce
1/2 cup prepared mincemeat
Powdered sugar

Preheat oven to 350°F (175°C). Butter an 8-inch square baking pan. Dust with flour and rotate pan to coat evenly. Shake out excess flour; set pan aside. Stir instant coffee powder into hot water to dissolve. In a medium bowl, combine flour, salt and baking soda. Cut in butter or margarine. Add molasses, eggs, and dissolved instant coffee powder. Beat well. Stir in applesauce and mincemeat. Pour into prepared pan. Bake in preheated oven 40 to 45 minutes. Turn out onto rack. Sprinkle with powdered sugar. Cut into 2-inch squares. Makes 16 squares.

Rumplemeyer Squares

Pudding mix makes an easy super-special treat.

1 (18.5-oz.) pkg. yellow cake mix
1 (3-3/4-oz.) pkg. instant vanilla pudding
   and pie filling mix
3/4 cup water
1/4 cup light rum or 1 teaspoon imitation
   rum flavoring plus 1/4 cup water

1/4 cup vegetable oil
1/2 cup chopped walnuts
Coffee-Rum Syrup, see below
Whipped cream, if desired
Chopped walnuts, if desired

Coffee-Rum Syrup:
1 cup brown sugar, firmly packed
1/2 cup water
2 tablespoons instant coffee powder

1 tablespoon rum or 1 teaspoon
   imitation rum flavoring

Preheat oven to 350°F (175°C). Butter a 13" x 9" baking pan. Dust with flour and rotate pan to coat evenly. Shake out excess flour; set pan aside. In a medium bowl, combine cake mix, pudding mix, water, rum or rum flavoring and oil. Blend, then beat with electric mixer on medium speed 2 minutes. Fold in walnuts. Pour into prepared pan. Bake in preheated oven 45 minutes or until top springs back when lightly touched with fingertips. Cool in pan on rack 15 minutes. Prepare Coffee-Rum Syrup. Poke holes in cake with a fork. Pour warm syrup over cake. Let stand 2 to 3 hours. Cut into squares. If desired, garnish with whipped cream and chopped walnuts. Makes 10 to 12 servings.

Coffee-Rum Syrup:
Combine brown sugar and water in a small saucepan. Stir over low heat until sugar dissolves. Bring to a boil, lower heat and simmer 5 minutes. Remove from heat. Stir in instant coffee powder and rum or rum flavoring. Cool 5 minutes.

Louisiana Brandied Fruitcake

Begin this cake a month ahead and really enjoy the holidays!

1-1/2 lbs. diced mixed candied fruits (3 cups)
1/2 lb. chopped pecans (2-1/2 cups)
1 (15-oz.) pkg. raisins
1/2 cup brandy
2 tablespoons butter or margarine,
   room temperature
2 tablespoons fine dry breadcrumbs
3 cups all-purpose flour
1 teaspoon baking powder

1/2 teaspoon salt
1/4 teaspoon ground allspice
1/2 teaspoon cinnamon
1 cup more butter or margarine (2 sticks),
   room temperature
2 cups light brown sugar, firmly packed
4 eggs
3/4 cup prepared coffee
2 cups more brandy

In a large bowl, combine candied fruits, pecans, raisins and 1/2 cup brandy. Stir to mix thoroughly. Cover and let stand 3 to 5 hours at room temperature. Preheat oven to 275°F (135°C). Butter two 9" x 5" loaf pans using 1 tablespoon butter or margarine for each. Sprinkle each with 1 tablespoon breadcrumbs and rotate pans to coat evenly; set pans aside. Sift together flour, baking powder, salt, allspice and cinnamon. In a large bowl, cream 1 cup butter or margarine with brown sugar. Add eggs. Beat until light and fluffy. Add flour mixture alternately with coffee, stirring after each addition until batter is just blended. Pour over fruit-nut mixture. Blend thoroughly. Spoon into prepared pans. Bake in preheated oven 1-1/2 hours until a wooden pick inserted in center comes out clean. Turn out onto racks. Cool completely. Sprinkle each cake with about 1/4 cup brandy. Wrap in aluminum foil and seal well. Store in a cool dark place. After 7 days, unwrap and sprinkle each cake with another 1/4 cup brandy. Rewrap. Repeat unwrapping and sprinkling with brandy each week for 2 weeks. Let cakes mellow a final week before serving. Makes two-9-inch loaf cakes.

To eliminate the messy and wasteful job of scraping butter or margarine from the paper, remove it from the refrigerator and unwrap it immediately. Place it in a bowl, lightly covered with the wrapping paper, to soften.

Walnut Squares

Walnuts, coffee and Apricot Sauce blend in a great taste.

1-1/2 cups cake flour
1 teaspoon cream of tartar
1 teaspoon baking powder
1 (4-oz.) pkg. ground walnuts (2/3 cup)
1/2 cup butter or margarine (1 stick),
   room temperature
1 cup sugar

2 whole eggs
3/4 cup prepared cold coffee
2 egg whites; reserve yolks for sauce
1/2 teaspoon baking soda dissolved in
   1 tablespoon water
Apricot Sauce, see below

Apricot Sauce:
1/4 cup sugar
2 egg yolks
2 tablespoons apricot jam

2 tablespoons kirsch liqueur or orange juice
1/2 teaspoon grated lemon peel
3/4 cup dairy sour cream

Preheat oven to 325°F (165°C). Oil a 13" x 9" baking pan and line with wax paper. Coat wax paper with oil, sprinkle evenly with flour and rotate pan to coat evenly. Shake out excess flour; set pan aside. Sift together flour, cream of tartar and baking powder. Add ground walnuts. Stir until thoroughly mixed. In a large bowl, cream butter or margarine with sugar until very light and fluffy. Blend in whole eggs. Add coffee alternately with flour-nut mixture, stirring well after each addition. Beat egg whites until stiff. Fold into batter. Stir in dissolved baking soda. Spoon batter into prepared pan and spread evenly. Bake in preheated oven 45 minutes or until top springs back when lightly touched with fingertips and cake shrinks slightly from sides of pan. Prepare Apricot Sauce. Cool cake in pan on rack. Cut into squares. Serve at room temperature or chilled. Spoon chilled Apricot Sauce over each serving. Makes 12 servings.

Apricot Sauce:

Combine sugar and egg yolks in top of double boiler over, not in, simmering water. Beat with electric or rotary beater until very thick and smooth. Remove pan from water and continue to beat until cooled. Stir in jam, liqueur or orange juice, lemon peel and sour cream. Place plastic wrap directly on surface of sauce. Cover and chill.

Sift dry ingredients onto a sheet of wax paper and you won't have to use an extra bowl.

Peanut Butter Bars

Penuche Icing adds the final delicious touch.

1-1/2 cups all-purpose flour
1/2 teaspoon baking soda
1 teaspoon baking powder
1/4 teaspoon salt
1/2 cup butter or margarine (1 stick),
   room temperature
3/4 cup sugar

1/2 cup creamy or crunchy peanut butter,
   room temperature
1 egg
2 tablespoons instant coffee powder dissolved
   in 1 tablespoon hot water
1 cup milk

Penuche Icing:

1/4 cup butter or margarine (1/2 stick)
1/2 cup brown sugar, firmly packed
2 tablespoons instant coffee powder dissolved
   in 1 tablespoon hot water

1 to 1-1/2 cups powdered sugar

Preheat oven to 350°F (175°C). Butter a 9-inch square baking pan. Dust with flour and rotate pan to coat evenly. Shake out excess flour; set pan aside. Sift together flour, baking soda, baking powder and salt. In a medium bowl, cream butter or margarine with sugar and peanut butter. Stir in egg and dissolved instant coffee powder. Fold flour mixture and milk into batter alternately. Blend thoroughly. Pour into prepared pan. Bake in preheated oven 25 to 30 minutes or until top springs back when lightly touched with fingertips. Cool in pan on rack. Prepare Penuche Icing. Spread on cake in pan. Cut cake into 2-1/2" x 3" bars and remove from pan with spatula. Makes 12 bars.

Penuche Icing:

Melt butter or margarine in a medium saucepan over low heat. Add brown sugar and dissolved instant coffee powder. Stir until brown sugar dissolves. Remove from heat. Add 1 cup powdered sugar. Blend until smooth. Add enough additional powdered sugar to bring mixture to spreading consistency.

Pies & Pastries

American cooks have always been famous for their pies and tarts. New England apple pies, pumpkin pie from the Midwest and the pecan and fruit pies of the South are all part of our culinary heritage.

Included in this book are traditional favorites: Glazed Apple Pie, a very special Praline-Pumpkin Pie, Brown Sugar Pie from an old Charleston recipe, Heavenly Hash tarts from New Orleans and Mincemeat Tarts. The rich flavor of these favorites is heightened with coffee.

The pies in this book are easy to make. You can use the excellent quality frozen pie and tart shells available in most supermarkets. However, if you want to master the art of homemade pastry, don't hesitate. It's far easier than you think. The recipe on page 116 is a proven success. Making your own pastry is worth it if only for your own pleasure and sense of accomplishment. The two main causes of tough pastry are using too much flour when rolling out the crust and too much handling of the dough. It's easier for me to get the thin, light texture I want in pastry by using a pastry cloth and a cotton mit for my rolling pin. The dough rolls out easier and requires less flour to keep from sticking.

Hearty Supper for a Cold Winter Night
Meat Loaf Ring With
Mashed Potatoes & Vegetables, page 26
Tossed Green Salad
Brown Sugar Pie, page 110
Spiced Coffee With Coffee Cream, page 14

Grasshopper Pie

An easy spectacular dessert for your next dinner party.

1 tablespoon butter or margarine
1/2 cup more butter or margarine (1 stick)

1-1/2 cups chocolate cookie wafer crumbs
1/2 cup powdered sugar

Peppermint-Lime Filling:
1 (3-oz.) pkg. lime gelatin
2 tablespoons sugar
1 cup boiling water
1/2 cup cold water
1/2 teaspoon peppermint extract
1 envelope unflavored gelatin
1/4 cup more cold water
1 cup more boiling water

2 tablespoons instant coffee powder
1/4 cup more sugar
1/2 teaspoon vanilla extract
1/2 cup cold milk
2 envelopes whipped topping mix
1/2 cup more cold milk
1/2 teaspoon vanilla extract
Instant coffee powder for garnish

Coat a 9-inch pie plate with 1 tablespoon butter or margarine. Melt 1/2 cup butter or margarine in a large skillet. Stir in cookie crumbs and powdered sugar. Press firmly into pie plate. Refrigerate until firm.

Peppermint-Lime Filling:
Combine lime gelatin and 2 tablespoons sugar in a small bowl. Pour in 1 cup boiling water. Stir to dissolve gelatin and sugar. Stir in 1/2 cup cold water and peppermint extract. Refrigerate until thickened. In a medium bowl, sprinkle unflavored gelatin over 1/4 cup cold water. Add 1 cup boiling water, 2 tablespoons instant coffee powder, 1/4 cup sugar and vanilla extract. Refrigerate until thickened. Combine 1/2 cup cold milk and 1 envelope whipped topping mix in a deep narrow bowl. Beat until peaks form when beaters are lifted from bowl; beat 2 minutes longer or until light and fluffy. Chill. Fold chilled topping into thickened coffee gelatin. Beat until smooth. Pour into prepared pie shell. Pour thickened lime gelatin on top. Refrigerate pie until firm. Prepare whipped topping with 1 envelope whipped topping mix, 1/2 cup cold milk and 1/2 teaspoon vanilla extract. Just before serving, top pie with whipped topping. If desired, sprinkle with instant coffee powder. Makes one 9-inch pie.

For best results, use the exact size pie or tart shells the recipe calls for.

Nesselrode Pie

Gourmet departments in supermarkets often carry Nesselrode sauce.

1 envelope unflavored gelatin
1/4 cup prepared cold coffee
1/2 cup prepared hot coffee
1 tablespoon instant coffee powder
1/2 cup sugar
2 tablespoons rum or 1/2 teaspoon
   imitation rum flavoring

1/2 pint whipping cream
3/4 cup bottled Nesselrode sauce
1 (9-inch) pie shell, baked and cooled
Whipped cream, if desired

In top of double boiler, sprinkle gelatin over cold coffee. Let stand 5 minutes to soften. Add hot coffee, instant coffee powder and sugar. Stir over, not in, simmering water until gelatin and sugar dissolve. Remove pan from hot water. Stir in rum or rum flavoring. Cool slightly. Place pan in a larger pan of ice water. Whip until mixture begins to thicken to a custard. Beat cream in a large bowl until stiff. Fold in custard and Nesselrode sauce. Spoon into baked pie shell. Refrigerate until firm. If desired, garnish with whipped cream just before serving. Makes one 9-inch pie.

Mocha-Mallow Pie

Marshmallows, cocoa and coffee in a superb creamy filling.

24 marshmallows
3/4 cup prepared coffee
2 tablespoons cocoa powder
Pinch of salt
1 envelope unflavored gelatin

1/4 cup cold water
1/2 pint dairy sour cream
1 (9-inch) pie shell, baked and cooled
Sweet Rum Topping, see below
Candy coffee beans, if desired

Sweet Rum Topping:
1/2 pint whipping cream
1/3 cup powdered sugar

1 tablespoon rum or 1 teaspoon
   imitation rum flavoring

Place marshmallows, coffee, cocoa powder and salt in top of double boiler over, not in, simmering water. Stir until marshmallows melt and mixture is smooth. Remove pan from hot water. In a small saucepan, sprinkle gelatin over cold water. Stir over low heat until gelatin dissolves and mixture is clear. Stir into marshmallow mixture. Cool to room temperature. Fold in sour cream. Pour into baked pie shell. Chill. Prepare Sweet Rum Topping. Spread over surface of chilled pie. Sprinkle with coffee candy beans, if desired. Makes one 9-inch pie.

Sweet Rum Topping:
In a small bowl, beat cream until stiff. Fold in sugar and rum or rum flavoring.

Praline-Pumpkin Pie

Extra-special pumpkin pie filling makes picture-pretty tarts.

2 tablespoons apricot jam
1 teaspoon brandy or water
1 (9-inch) unbaked deep-dish pie shell or
   10 (3-inch) tart shells, 1 inch deep
3/4 cup chopped pecans
1 (1-lb.) can cooked pumpkin
1 (14-oz.) can sweetened condensed milk
1/4 cup more brandy

2 tablespoons instant coffee powder
1/3 cup granulated sugar
1 egg, slightly beaten
1/4 teaspoon ginger
1/4 teaspoon cinnamon
1/4 teaspoon nutmeg
1/4 cup more chopped pecans
1/2 cup brown sugar, firmly packed

Place jam and 1 teaspoon brandy or water in a heatproof measuring cup. Place cup in pan of hot water. Stir mixture to a smooth syrupy glaze. Remove from heat and set aside. Preheat oven to 425°F (220°C). With a fork, prick bottom of pie shell or tart shells in several places. Line with aluminum foil, shiny side down. Bake in preheated oven 15 minutes. Remove foil and cool slightly. With a pastry brush, spread apricot syrup over bottom of shell. Return it to oven 2 minutes. Remove from oven. Sprinkle with 3/4 cup chopped pecans; set pie shell aside. Reduce oven temperature to 350°F (175°C). In a medium bowl, combine pumpkin, condensed milk, 1/4 cup brandy, instant coffee powder, granulated sugar, egg, ginger, cinnamon and nutmeg. Beat until blended. Spoon into pie shell or tart shells over nuts. Bake in preheated oven 45 to 50 minutes or until knife inserted in center comes out clean. Sprinkle with 1/4 cup chopped pecans and brown sugar. Cover pie edges with aluminum foil. Place about 3 inches under high broiler heat 1 minute or until sugar bubbles. Cool. Gently crack topping with tip of knife before cutting. Makes one 9-inch pie or ten 3-inch tarts.

Brown Sugar Pie

Luscious and velvety with just a touch of spice.

3/4 cup brown sugar, firmly packed
3/4 cup granulated sugar
1/4 cup butter or margarine
1/4 cup whipping cream
1/4 cup prepared coffee

3 eggs, room temperature
1/2 teaspoon nutmeg
1 (9-inch) unbaked pie shell
Instant coffee powder for garnish
Whipped cream, if desired

Preheat oven to 450°F (230°C). Combine brown and granulated sugars, butter or margarine, cream and coffee in top of double boiler. Cook over, not in, simmering water, stirring occasionally, until sugar dissolves and butter or margarine melts. Beat eggs in a large bowl until thickened and lemon-colored. Gradually beat hot sugar mixture into eggs. Sprinkle nutmeg over bottom of pie shell. Fill with egg mixture. Bake in preheated oven 10 minutes. Reduce heat to 300°F (150°C) and bake 45 minutes more or until knife inserted in center comes out clean. While still hot, sprinkle with instant coffee powder. Serve chilled. Top with whipped cream if desired. Makes one 9-inch pie.

Glazed Apple Pie

An easy French-style version.

5 to 6 tart apples
1/2 cup brown sugar, firmly packed
2 teaspoons instant coffee powder
1 teaspoon apple pie spice

1 (9-inch) unbaked frozen pie shell
3 tablespoons granulated sugar
2 tablespoons butter or margarine,
   cut into slivers

Preheat oven to 450°F (230°C). Cut apples into quarters; remove core but do not peel. Cut quarters into thin slices. In a medium bowl, combine apples, brown sugar, instant coffee powder and apple pie spice. Blend well. Fill frozen pie shell with apple mixture. Bake in preheated oven 10 minutes. Reduce heat to 300°F (150°C) and bake 30 to 40 minutes more or until apples are tender. Sprinkle with granulated sugar and butter slivers 10 to 15 minutes before removing from oven. Makes one 9-inch pie.

Pineapple Cream Pie

Memories of ukuleles, Diamond Head and whispering surf.

1 envelope unflavored gelatin
1/4 cup cold water
1 (3-1/8-oz.) pkg. vanilla pudding and
   pie filling mix
1 cup prepared coffee
1/2 cup milk

1 (8-1/4-oz.) can crushed pineapple
   in heavy syrup, drained; reserve 1/2 cup
   syrup for topping
1/2 cup whipping cream
12 lady fingers
Pineapple Cream Topping, see below

Pineapple Cream Topping:
1 envelope unflavored gelatin
1/4 cup cold water

1/2 cup reserved syrup from crushed pineapple
1/2 cup whipping cream

In top of double boiler, sprinkle gelatin over cold water. Stir over, not in, simmering water until gelatin dissolves and mixture is clear. Prepare pudding mix according to package directions, using coffee and milk for the required liquid. Stir dissolved gelatin into hot pudding. Stir in drained crushed pineapple. Place plastic wrap directly on surface of pudding. Refrigerate until thickened but not set. Whip cream until stiff. Fold into thickened pudding. Split lady fingers in half. Line bottom of a 10-inch pie plate with 12 lady finger halves. Cut remaining halves in half again crosswise. Stand against sides of pie plate, rounded ends up to make a rim. Carefully spoon filling into pie plate. Refrigerate until firm. Prepare Pineapple Cream Topping. Spoon over surface of chilled pie. Makes one 10-inch pie.

Pineapple Cream Topping:

In a small saucepan, sprinkle gelatin over cold water. Stir over low heat until gelatin dissolves. Stir in pineapple syrup. Bring to a boil. Refrigerate until slightly thickened. In a chilled medium bowl, whip cream until stiff. Fold in gelatin mixture.

Cookie Pie

Ready-made cookies and coffee team up for a special dessert.

9 Pepperidge Farm Open Hearth Cookies
   or shortbread cookies
4 eggs
1/2 cup sugar
1 cup prepared coffee
1 envelope unflavored gelatin

1/4 cup cold water
1 cup whipping cream
1/2 cup brown sugar, firmly packed
1 teaspoon instant coffee powder
Whipped cream for garnish, if desired

Arrange cookies around the bottom of a 9-inch glass pie plate to form a circle. Place 1 cookie in the center; set aside. Combine eggs and sugar in top of a double boiler over, not in, simmering water. Beat to blend well. Add coffee. Stir frequently until custard thickens and coats a wooden spoon. Remove pan from hot water. Sprinkle gelatin over cold water; let stand 5 minutes to soften. Add to hot custard. Stir until completely dissolved. Cool custard to room temperature. Beat cream until stiff. Fold into custard. Pour over cookies in pie plate. Refrigerate until firm. Combine brown sugar and instant coffee powder in a small saucepan. Stir over very low heat until sugar is almost melted. Remove from heat. Cool slightly. Sprinkle over surface of pie. Serve cold. Garnish with whipped cream, if desired. Makes one 9-inch pie.

Kentucky Colonel's Chiffon Pie

Kentucky cooks really know how to make pies.

1 (9-inch) Graham Cracker Crumb Crust,
   page 116
1 envelope unflavored gelatin
1/4 cup cold water
4 egg yolks
1 cup light brown sugar, firmly packed

2 tablespoons instant coffee powder
1/4 cup bourbon
4 egg whites
1/2 cup granulated sugar
2 tablespoons graham cracker crumbs

Prepare Graham Cracker Crumb Crust; set aside. Sprinkle gelatin over cold water in a small bowl; let stand 5 minutes to soften. Combine egg yolks and brown sugar in top of double boiler over, not in, simmering water. Beat with electric or rotary beater until about tripled in volume. Add instant coffee powder. Beat until blended. Stir in softened gelatin. Beat 30 seconds. Remove pan from hot water. Stir in bourbon. Cool to room temperature. Beat egg whites until almost stiff. Add granulated sugar a little at a time; continue to beat until very thick and stiff. Fold about 1/3 of the beaten egg whites into the egg yolk mixture, then fold egg yolk mixture into remaining egg white mixture. Pour into prepared Graham Cracker Crumb Crust. Sprinkle with graham cracker crumbs. Chill. Makes one 9-inch pie.

Easy Black Bottom Pie

Something different in both the crust and the filling.

3 (1.3-oz.) chocolate-covered peanut
    candy bars, broken in small pieces
2 tablespoons instant coffee powder
1/3 cup peanut butter
1 cup chocolate cookie wafer crumbs

3 tablespoons butter or margarine,
    room temperature
Lemon Filling, see below
Chocolate cookie wafer crumbs for garnish

Lemon Filling:
1-1/2 cups milk
1 envelope whipped topping mix
1 (3-3/4-oz.) pkg. lemon instant pudding
    and pie filling mix

1 teaspoon grated lemon peel

Generously butter a 9-inch pie plate. Combine candy bars, instant coffee powder and peanut butter in top of double boiler over, not in, simmering water. Stir until candy melts and mixture is blended. Remove pan from hot water. Stir in 1 cup cookie crumbs and butter or margarine. Refrigerate until thickened but not hardened. With fingers press into prepared pie plate to form a pie shell. Chill in freezer 10 minutes. Prepare Lemon Filling. Spoon into pie shell. Refrigerate 3 hours or longer. Garnish with cookie crumbs. Makes one 9-inch pie.

Lemon Filling:
Blend milk, whipped topping mix and pudding mix in a medium bowl. Blend then beat with electric mixer on high speed 5 minutes or until thickened.

Peaches & Cream Pie

A glorious dessert!

2-1/2 cups peeled and sliced frozen
    or fresh peaches
1/2 cup brown sugar, firmly packed
1 tablespoon instant coffee powder
1 teaspoon tapioca
1/4 teaspoon cinnamon

1/4 teaspoon nutmeg
4 tablespoons dairy sour cream
1 (9-inch) unbaked pie shell
3/4 cup more dairy sour cream
1/4 cup more brown sugar,
    firmly packed

Preheat oven to 400°F (205°C). In a medium bowl, combine sliced peaches, brown sugar, instant coffee powder, tapioca, cinnamon, nutmeg and 4 tablespoons sour cream. Toss to mix well. Spoon into unbaked pie shell. Bake in preheated oven 10 minutes. Reduce heat to 350°F (175°C) and continue to bake 20 to 25 mintues or until crust is golden and filling is thickened. Top with 3/4 cup sour cream and sprinkle with 1/4 cup brown sugar. Serve warm. Makes one 9-inch pie.

How To Make Easy Black Bottom Pie

1/Break up candy bars before melting with instant coffee powder and peanut butter in top of double boiler. Stir in cookie crumbs and butter or margarine. Refrigerate until mixture thickens.

2/Press thickened mixture into buttered pie plate. Place in freezer 10 minutes while preparing Lemon Filling.

3/Spoon Lemon Filling into pie shell. Chill pie. Before serving, garnish with chocolate cookie crumbs.

Perfect Pie Crust

For best results, mix dough in the morning, refrigerate it and make the pie in the afternoon.

1-1/2 cups all-purpose flour
6 tablespoons cold butter or margarine
   (3/4 stick), cut in slivers
2 tablespoons vegetable shortening

1/8 teaspoon salt
2 tablespoons sugar
3 to 5 tablespoons ice water

Combine all ingredients except ice water in a large bowl. Toss to blend. Work the mixture with pastry blender or fingers until it resembles coarse meal. Sprinkle with about 3 tablespoons ice water. Mix quickly, then gather dough into a ball. If necessary, add enough additional ice water 1 tablespoon at a time to just hold dough together. Wrap in foil or plastic wrap and refrigerate several hours. On a lightly floured surface, roll out to about 1/8 inch thick. Fold in half; place in a 9-inch pie plate. Bake according to pie recipe directions. If recipe calls for prebaked pie shell, bake in preheated 450°F (230°C) oven 10 to 12 minutes or until lightly browned. Makes 1 single 9-inch crust or 6 to 8 individual tart shells.

Graham Cracker Crumb Crust

Perfect for Kentucky Colonel's Chiffon Pie, page 113.

1 teaspoon butter or margarine,
   room temperature
4 tablespoons more butter or margarine

1 cup graham cracker crumbs (12 crackers)
2 tablespoons powdered sugar

Preheat oven to 300°F (150°C). Coat a 9-inch pie plate with 1 teaspoon butter or margarine. In a medium skillet over low heat, melt 4 tablespoons butter or margarine. Cool. Stir in graham cracker crumbs and powdered sugar. Spread and press mixture on bottom and sides of prepared pie plate. Bake in preheated oven 15 minutes. Cool before filling. Makes one 9-inch pie shell.

To prevent a soggy bottom crust when making a fruit or custard pie, brush a little beaten egg on the crust and chill before filling.

Heavenly Hash Tarts

Walnuts, raisins and coffee blend in this delicious and authentic southern recipe.

1/2 cup butter or margarine (1 stick),
   room temperature
1 cup light brown sugar, firmly packed
1/2 cup prepared coffee
1-1/2 tablespoons all-purpose flour
1/2 cup chopped walnuts

1/2 cup raisins
1 tablespoon rum or brandy, if desired
8 (3-inch) frozen tart shells, 1 inch deep
Dairy sour cream or vanilla ice cream,
   if desired

Preheat oven to 450°F (230°C). In a small bowl, cream butter or margarine with brown sugar until light and fluffy. Stir in coffee. Combine flour, walnuts and raisins in a small bowl. Add to sugar mixture. Add rum or brandy. Blend well. Fill still-frozen tart shells about 3/4 full. Bake on baking sheet in preheated oven 10 minutes. Reduce oven temperature to 300°F (150°C). Bake 15 to 20 minutes or until crust is deep golden brown. Remove from baking sheet. Cool on rack at least 30 minutes. Serve warm or cold. Filling will sink in center as tarts cool. Fill center with sour cream or ice cream, if desired. Makes 8 tarts.

Mincemeat Tarts

Warm mellow tarts with a sweet rich sauce.

Lemony Hard Sauce, see below
2 tablespoons instant coffee powder
1/4 cup brandy

Lemony Hard Sauce:
4 tablespoons butter or margarine,
   room temperature
1 cup powdered sugar
1 tablespoon brandy

1 medium, tart apple, peeled and chopped
2 cups prepared mincemeat
8 (3-inch) frozen tart shells, 1 inch deep

1/4 cup whipping cream
1 teaspoon grated lemon peel

Prepare Lemony Hard Sauce; chill. Preheat oven to 450°F (230°C). Dissolve instant coffee powder in brandy. In a medium bowl, combine chopped apple, mincemeat and coffee-brandy mixture. Spoon into still-frozen tart shells. Bake in preheated oven 10 minutes. Reduce heat to 350°F (175°C) and bake 20 minutes. Serve warm topped with Lemony Hard Sauce. Makes 8 tarts.

Lemony Hard Sauce:
In a small bowl, cream butter or margarine with powdered sugar. Stir in brandy. Add cream. Beat until light and fluffy. Fold in lemon peel. Cover and refrigerate until chilled.

How To Make Almond Cream Horns

1/Wrap a buttered strip of aluminum foil smoothly around each cone. Buttered side of foil should face out.

2/Roll out each cold patty shell to an 11″ x 9″ rectangle. Trim the edges and cut each rectangle in half to make two 5-1/2″ x 9″ strips.

3/Wrap each strip of pastry around a foil-covered cone. Slightly overlap the pastry edges, pressing lightly as you wrap.

Almond Cream Horns

Be the first to serve these elegant pastries!

10 cone-shaped ice cream cones
   for horn molds
5 frozen patty shells, thawed but cold

1 egg, slightly beaten
Almond Cream, see below

Almond Cream:
2 (3-3/4-oz.) pkgs. vanilla instant pudding and
   pie filling mix
2 cups milk

1/2 cup prepared coffee
1/2 teaspoon almond extract
1/4 cup slivered toasted almonds

Cut aluminum foil into ten 5-1/2" x 9" strips. Butter each strip. Wrap 1 strip buttered-side-out around each ice cream cone to make a neat smooth covering. Cut cold patty shells in half. On a lightly floured surface, roll out 1 at a time to an 11" x 9" rectangle about 1/8 inch thick. Trim edges and cut in half to make two 5-1/2" x 9" strips. Starting at the point of the cone, wrap each pastry strip around the foil-covered cones, slightly overlapping the edges of the pastry. Brush with egg. Stand pastry-wrapped cones upside down on a tray, not touching. Place in freezer 1/2 hour. Prepare Almond Cream; chill. Preheat oven to 450°F (230°C). Bake pastry-wrapped cones on baking sheet in preheated oven 10 to 15 minutes or until puffed and golden. Cool on racks. Carefully remove foil-wrapped cones from pastry horns and discard. Just before serving, fill pastry horns with chilled Almond Cream. Makes 10 servings.

Almond Cream:
Prepare pudding according to package directions using milk and coffee for the required liquid. Stir in almond extract and slivered almonds. Chill before filling cones.

4/Brush each pastry with beaten egg before placing on a tray in the freezer for 1/2 hour.

5/Bake pastries, still wrapped around cones, until puffed and golden. Cool completely before removing foil-covered cones and filling pastries with Almond Cream.

Dessert Sauces

The dessert sauces in this book are so unusual and delicious they can turn plain ice cream into a gala dessert or top an elegant dessert soufflé with an even more elegant flourish. Mocha Fondue is really a dessert in itself and as much fun to make as it is to eat.

These sauce recipes are so easy that few special instructions are necessary. You will find everything easier with a wire whisk and a wooden spoon.

You can prepare Peanut Butter Sauce or Orange Coffee Sauce ahead and store them in the refrigerator where they'll be on hand ready to transform a simple dessert into something special.

During the holidays, Coffee Hard Sauce is as welcome on slices of fruit cake or wedges of mince pie as it is on the usual plum pudding. It keeps well in the refrigerator so double or triple the recipe and you'll have plenty for festive occasions.

Zesty Hamburger Feast

Western-Style Hamburgers With
Chili Sauce, page 25
Avocado & Grapefruit Salad
Coffee Ice Cream With
Peanut Butter Sauce, page 121
Café au Lait, page 8

Mint-Coffee Sauce

Perfect for an ice cream buffet with a choice of other sauces and several ice cream flavors.

1/2 lb. chocolate peppermint patties
3 tablespoons instant coffee powder

1/4 cup whipping cream

In top of double boiler over, not in, simmering water, combine peppermint patties and instant coffee powder. Stir occasionally until patties are melted. Stir in cream. Blend well. Serve warm. Makes about 1-1/2 cups sauce.

Peanut Butter Sauce

Try it over coffee ice cream!

1 cup sugar
1 tablespoon cornstarch
1 tablespoon white corn syrup
1/4 teaspoon salt

3/4 cup prepared coffee
1/2 cup peanut butter, room temperature
1/2 teaspoon vanilla extract

In a small saucepan, combine sugar, cornstarch, corn syrup, salt and coffee. Stir over low heat until sugar dissolves. Stir in peanut butter. Continue to stir over low heat until sauce thickens and is smooth. Stir in vanilla extract. Serve warm. Sauce may be made ahead and reheated. Makes about 2 cups sauce.

Rum-Butter Sauce

Create a party parfait with pistachio ice cream layered with this creamy sauce.

1/2 cup sugar
3/4 cup prepared hot coffee
1 tablespoon cornstarch
2 tablespoons prepared cold coffee

1 tablespoon butter or margarine,
   room temperature
2 tablespoons rum

Place sugar in a saucepan over low heat. Stir often until dissolved to a light golden syrup. Add hot coffee slowly, stirring constantly until blended. Mix cornstarch with cold coffee. Stir into sugar mixture. Continue stirring over low heat until sauce thickens. Remove from heat. Add butter or margarine and rum. Stir until butter or margarine is melted. Makes about 1 cup sauce.

Double-Quick Ice Cream Sauce

The perfect sauce for Chocolate-Espresso Soufflé, page 131.

1 pint coffee ice cream
2 tablespoons instant coffee powder
2 tablespoons hot water

1/4 cup Alice Hastings Coffee Liqueur,
  page 156, or other coffee liqueur

In a medium bowl, soften ice cream slightly. Dissolve instant coffee powder in hot water. Pour liqueur over ice cream. Add dissolved coffee. Beat to consistency of whipped cream. Makes about 2 cups sauce.

Sweetened Whipped Cream

Sometimes called Crème Chantilly, it's delicious over gelatins, puddings and frozen desserts.

1 cup whipping cream
1 to 3 tablespoons sifted powdered sugar

1/2 teaspoon vanilla extract

Chill beaters and a small bowl in freezer. In chilled bowl, whip cream with cold beaters until stiff. Fold in powdered sugar and vanilla extract. Makes about 2 cups whipped cream.

Coffee Hard Sauce

Something different for traditional plum pudding or on Holiday Mincemeat Pudding, page 71.

1 cup butter or margarine,
  room temperature
1 cup powdered sugar

1 tablespoon instant coffee powder
1/4 cup brandy or rum

In a small bowl, cream butter or margarine with powdered sugar until light and fluffy. Add instant coffee powder and brandy or rum. Blend well. Pack into a 1-pint decorative mold. Chill until serving time. Unmold onto serving plate. Surround with holly leaves, if desired. Makes about 2 cups sauce.

Orange Coffee Sauce

Top sponge cake squares with this flavorful blend of orange and coffee.

3 tablespoons butter or margarine,
   room temperature
1/3 cup powdered sugar
2 tablespoons instant coffee powder

2 tablespoons hot water
1/2 pint whipping cream
2 tablespoons orange liqueur or orange juice
1 teaspoon grated orange peel

In a small bowl, cream butter or margarine with powdered sugar. Dissolve instant coffee powder in hot water. Add to creamed mixture. Beat until light and fluffy. Beat cream until stiff. Fold into coffee mixture. Add orange liqueur or orange juice and orange peel. Blend well. Chill. Makes about 2 cups sauce.

How To Make Orange Coffee Sauce

1/Cream butter or margarine with powdered sugar in a small bowl before beating in dissolved instant coffee powder.

2/Fold in stiffly beaten cream, orange liqueur or juice and peel. Blend well. Serve chilled over plain cake.

Mocha Fondue

Provide each guest with a skewer or fondue fork and dip in!

2 tablespoons instant coffee powder
1/4 cup boiling water
2 tablespoons butter or margarine,
  room temperature
12 (1-oz.) squares semisweet chocolate

1 angel food cake,
  cut in bite-size squares
1 (13-1/4-oz.) can unsweetened pineapple
  chunks, well drained
1 (4-oz.) jar maraschino cherries

Dissolve instant coffee powder in boiling water. Melt butter or margarine with chocolate in fondue pot, electric skillet or chafing dish over low heat. Stir in dissolved coffee. Keep warm. Spear cake squares, pineapple chunks and maraschino cherries with fondue forks. Dip into warm fondue and swirl to coat. Serve with small cups of strong black coffee. Makes about 2 cups fondue, enough for 6 to 8 servings.

Jamaican Rum Sauce

Enjoy slices of frozen pound cake topped with delicious sauce.

1 cup brown sugar, firmly packed
1-1/2 cups prepared hot coffee
2 tablespoons cornstarch
3 tablespoons rum or
  1 teaspoon imitation rum flavoring plus
  3 tablespoons water

2 tablespoons butter or margarine,
  room temperature

In a small saucepan, combine brown sugar and coffee. Stir over low heat until sugar melts. Blend cornstarch with rum or rum flavoring plus water. Stir into sugar-coffee mixture. Continue to stir over low heat until sauce boils and thickens. Remove from heat. Add butter or margarine. Stir until melted. Serve warm over ice cream, cake, pudding or custard. Makes about 2 cups sauce.

Dessert Soufflés

The word *soufflé* sounds mysterious to most of us. In reality, a soufflé is a simple mixture of flour, butter, sugar, liquid, egg yolks, beaten egg whites and flavoring. Although it's better for the guests to wait for the soufflé than the soufflé to wait for the guests, culinary history has more sad cases of soggy pastry than fallen soufflés.

If you want to add height to your soufflé mold, you can make your own *collar*. Cut a piece of wax paper or aluminum foil 12 inches wide and slightly longer than the rim of the mold. Fold into thirds. Butter 1 side and wrap around the outside of the mold, buttered-side in, overlapping the ends. The collar should extend about 2 inches above the mold. Secure with a piece of string wrapped around the mold and tied.

Don't pay any attention to the myth that a soufflé will fall the moment it's taken from the oven. A well-baked soufflé prepared from a good recipe will stand up 15 to 20 minutes.

Enjoy the flavor coffee adds to these gourmet desserts. If you've never made a soufflé before, start with the Brazilian Soufflé. Top it with a sprinkle of powdered sugar and a swirl of whipped cream. You'll be delighted with the result.

Many soufflés improve when served with a sauce. You'll find several sauces to choose from in the section on Dessert Sauces, page 120. Or pass a bowl of Sweetened Whipped Cream, page 122, flavored with a tablespoon or two of coffee and just a touch of liqueur.

Distinctive Dinner For Four

Coffee-Glazed Duck, page 29
Freshly Cooked Rice
With Tiny Peas &
Water Chestnut Slices
Boston Lettuce Salad With
Camembert Cheese
Brazilian Soufflé, page 127
Café Crème de Cacao, page 156

Brazilian Soufflé

South America influences a continental favorite.

2 tablespoons butter or margarine
1-1/2 tablespoons all-purpose flour
2 tablespoons instant coffee powder
1/2 cup hot milk
1 tablespoon Grand Marnier liqueur or
   other orange liqueur

5 eggs, separated
5 tablespoons sugar
1/4 cup slivered Brazil nuts
1 tablespoon more sugar
Whipped cream

Preheat oven to 350°F (175°C). Generously butter a 1-quart soufflé mold or casserole dish. Sprinkle with sugar and rotate to coat sides and bottom evenly. Refrigerate. Melt butter or margarine in a medium saucepan over low heat. Add flour. Stir over low heat 4 to 5 minutes. Dissolve instant coffee power in hot milk. Slowly add to flour mixture. Stir constantly over low heat until smooth and thick. Stir in liqueur. Remove from heat. Beat egg yolks with 3 tablespoons of the sugar until thickened and lemon-colored. Stir into milk-flour base. Beat egg whites until frothy. Add the 2 remaining tablespoons sugar. Beat until peaks form when beaters are lifted from bowl. Fold into soufflé base. Pour into prepared mold. Roll slivered Brazil nuts in 1 tablespoon of sugar. Sprinkle over soufflé. Bake in preheated oven 40 to 45 minutes. Serve at once with cold whipped cream. Makes 6 servings.

Tips For a Perfect Soufflé

Eggs separate more easily when they are cold, but beat to a greater volume at room temperature. If your recipe calls for well-beaten egg whites or yolks, separate them into 2 bowls while cold and cover bowls with plastic wrap. Let stand until they warm to room temperature for easier beating.

When making a soufflé, the butter-flour-sugar base should be beaten creamy smooth when cooled to room temperature before adding the lightly beaten egg yolks.

The best tool for beating soufflés is a wire whisk. Use it to beat the lightly beaten egg yolks into the soufflé base then wash and dry the whisk thoroughly before using it to beat the egg whites.

Don't overbeat egg whites. Beat them until stiff but still glossy, never until dry. Underbeating makes a soufflé small and unstable. Overbeating makes it tough.

Fold the stiffly beaten egg whites into the soufflé base very gently to retain the air beaten into the egg whites. This helps make an impressively light soufflé.

Walnut Soufflé Roll

Make this rich and beautiful dessert in the morning and be ready for your dinner party tonight.

6 egg whites
5 egg yolks
1/2 cup granulated sugar
1/2 teaspoon vanilla extract
1 cup ground walnuts
Mocha Filling, see below

Whipped Cream Filling, see below
Powdered sugar for garnish
Instant coffee powder for garnish
Sweetened Whipped Cream, page 122,
   if desired

Mocha Filling:

2 (1-oz.) squares unsweetened chocolate
3 tablespoons instant coffee powder

1/2 cup sugar
1 egg yolk

Whipped Cream Filling:

1/2 envelope unflavored gelatin
1/4 cup prepared cold coffee
1/2 pint whipping cream

1/2 cup powdered sugar
1/2 teaspoon imitation walnut flavoring

Preheat oven to 350°F (175°C). Butter a 15" x 10" jelly roll pan or a baking sheet with shallow sides. Line with wax paper leaving a 2-inch overhang at each end; butter wax paper. Set pan aside. In a large bowl, beat egg whites with electric mixer on high speed until stiff peaks form when beaters are lifted from bowl. In top of double boiler, combine egg yolks and 1/2 cup granulated sugar. Place over, not in, very hot water on low heat. Beat until pale lemon-colored and about doubled in volume. Remove from water. Stir in vanilla extract. Fold in about 1/4 of the beaten egg whites. Fold egg yolk mixture into remaining whites. Quickly fold in ground walnuts. Pour into prepared pan and spread mixture evenly to pan edges. Bake on center rack of preheated oven 18 to 20 minutes or until surface springs back when lightly touched with fingertips. Sprinkle a long sheet of wax paper or aluminum foil evenly with powdered sugar. Turn soufflé out onto wax paper or foil. Carefully roll up warm soufflé into a neat roll. Cool. Prepare Mocha and Whipped Cream Fillings. Unroll soufflé and spread with Mocha Filling and then with Whipped Cream Filling. Again roll up souffle. Slide seam-side down onto a long serving platter or a foil-covered breadboard. Refrigerate until serving time. Just before serving, sprinkle with powdered sugar and instant coffee powder. To serve, cut with a sharp knife into thick slices. If desired, top each slice with Sweetened Whipped Cream. Makes 8 to 12 servings.

Mocha Filling:
Combine all ingredients in top of double boiler over, not in, simmering water. Stir until very thick and smooth, about 5 minutes. Remove from heat and cool to room temperature.

Whipped Cream Filling:
In a heatproof cup or small saucepan, sprinkle gelatin into cold coffee. Let stand 5 minutes to soften. Whip cream until stiff. Fold in powdered sugar and walnut flavoring. Place gelatin-coffee mixture over low heat until gelatin completely dissolves. Fold into whipped cream.

How To Make Walnut Soufflé Roll

1/While soufflé is baking, sprinkle a long sheet of wax paper or aluminum foil with powdered sugar. Turn soufflé out onto powdered sugar and roll up with wax paper or foil into a neat roll. Cool and unroll.

2/Spread soufflé with a layer of Mocha Filling and a layer of Whipped Cream Filling.

3/Roll up soufflé again—this time without the wax paper or foil. Slide onto a serving platter and refrigerate until ready to serve.

Frozen Almond Soufflé

Another cold soufflé comes to the aid of the plan-ahead cook.

9 egg yolks
3/4 cup sugar
3 tablespoons instant coffee powder
1/3 cup almond liqueur or
    prepared coffee plus
    1 teaspoon almond extract

2 cups finely crushed almond macaroons
1 pint whipping cream
1 to 2 tablespoons more
    crushed almond macaroons

Wrap a 1-quart soufflé mold or casserole dish with a lightly buttered aluminum foil collar 2 inches higher than rim of mold. Hold in place with tape. Place mold in freezer. Combine egg yolks and sugar in top of double boiler over, not in, simmering water. Beat with electric or rotary beater until tripled in volume. Dissolve instant coffee powder in liqueur or coffee and almond extract. Stir into egg yolk mixture. Remove pan from hot water. Stir in crushed macaroons. Place wax paper directly on surface of custard mixture. Chill. In a medium bowl, beat cream until stiff. Fold in chilled custard. Pour into prepared mold. Freeze 8 hours or longer. Gently remove collar from soufflé. Just before serving, sprinkle with 1 to 2 tablespoons crushed macaroons and gently press into soufflé. Makes 8 to 10 servings.

Plan Ahead

Here's how you can serve a hot soufflé without your dinner guests fidgeting with delay. Prepare the soufflé base and mold ahead, place the egg whites in a bowl to come to room temperature, and preheat the oven. Excuse yourself from your guests for no more than 10 minutes about 30 to 40 minutes before dessert is to be served, whip the egg whites to stiff peaks, fold them into the base, pour the whole thing into the prepared soufflé mold and slide it into the oven. It will rise to glorious heights while you enjoy your guests and the rest of the meal.

Chocolate-Espresso Soufflé

Delicious with Double-Quick Ice Cream Sauce, page 122.

2 (1-oz.) squares semisweet chocolate	4 tablespoons all-purpose flour
1/4 cup water	1/2 teaspoon vanilla extract
3/4 cup milk	3 eggs, separated
3 tablespoons instant coffee powder	1/2 cup sugar
4 tablespoons butter or margarine	

Generously butter a 2-quart soufflé mold or casserole dish. Sprinkle with sugar and rotate mold to coat sides and bottom evenly. Refrigerate. Preheat oven to 350°F (175°C). In a small saucepan over low heat, melt chocolate with water. Stir until smooth. Stir in milk and instant coffee powder. Stir over low heat until steaming and blended. Remove from heat. In another saucepan, melt butter or margarine. Add flour. Stir over low heat until bubbly. Add chocolate mixture slowly, stirring constantly. Contine to stir over low heat until thickened. Cool. Stir in vanilla extract. In a large bowl, beat egg whites until soft peaks form when beaters are lifted from bowl. Fold in sugar 2 tablespoons at a time; continue to beat until stiff. Without washing beaters, beat egg yolks in a small bowl until light and lemon-colored. Fold first egg yolks then chocolate mixture into the egg whites. Spoon into prepared mold. Bake in preheated oven 45 minutes. Serve warm. Makes 6 to 8 servings.

Banana Soufflé

An easy version of an elegant dessert.

12 lady fingers	1/2 cup sugar
1/4 cup Alice Hasting's Coffee Liqueur, page 156, or other coffee liqueur	2 egg yolks
	1/4 cup more coffee liqueur
4 or 5 large bananas, enough to make 2 cups banana puree	2 tablespoons instant coffee powder
	3 egg whites
1 tablespoon cornstarch	

Preheat oven to 300°F (150°C). Butter a 1-quart soufflé mold or casserole dish. Split lady fingers. Sprinkle evenly with 1/4 cup liqueur. Cut off 1/3 of each lady finger half. Line the sides of mold with the longer pieces, rounded ends up. Cut shorter pieces into cubes. Line bottom of mold with cubes. Set mold aside. Peel and mash bananas to a smooth puree or puree in electric blender. In top of double boiler, combine cornstarch, sugar, egg yolks and 1/4 cup liqueur. Stir over, not in, simmering water until thickened and smooth. Remove pan from hot water and stir in banana puree and instant coffee powder. In a medium bowl, beat egg whites until stiff. Fold into coffee-banana base. Spoon into prepared mold. Bake in preheated oven 25 to 30 minutes or until top of soufflé is firm. Spoon into serving dishes. Serve warm or cold. Makes 6 to 8 servings.

Cookies & Candies

Is there any nicer after-dinner gesture than a tray of unique coffee candies served with cups of fragrant black coffee? For many hostesses this pleasant custom has replaced dessert entirely.

Homemade cookies and candies are also welcome gifts. And the ones in this book are no ordinary sugar crisps or familiar fudge, but really superb, unusual candies and cookies that are a new experience in confections.

Coffee is used in these recipes with a lavish hand to banish the bland cloying sweetness of many homemade sweets. Taste for yourself the perfect after dinner Coffee Mints or the Pecan Brittle. It tasted so good when tested, it vanished in minutes.

Candy and cookie making is so easy, yet so creative, the making itself can be a pleasurable hobby. You need very little special equipment and you probably already own that. Make sure you have a flat, shiny-surface cookie sheet. Cookies baked in a pan with a rim do not cook evenly and are apt to stick. For brownies and other cake-like cookies, a pan with sides about 1-1/2-inches high gives best results. Coat pans or sheets generously with butter or margarine and always fill completely and evenly, spacing cookies about 1 inch apart.

Be sure your oven is preheated to the correct temperature before you put the cookies in. Most cookies bake very fast, so stand by to remove them as soon as they are ready.

Candy making can be even easier than cookies if you follow a few simple rules.

• Use a candy thermometer. This small investment will repay you many times over by saving the loss of otherwise perfect candy that failed because it was either undercooked or overcooked.

• Always use a large heavy pot to avoid scorching and boil-overs—a cleanup job no one wants.

• Finally, arm yourself with a big wooden spoon. Nothing surpasses this humble tool for stirring and beating candy to perfection.

Teen Age Coffee Party

Walnut Brownies, page 140
Rocky Road Clusters, page 136
Mochachino, page 14
Cinnamon Cafe con Leche, page 17

Caramel Bars

A perfect sweet for afternoon coffee.

24 caramels (about 8-oz.)
2 tablespoons prepared coffee
1/2 cup butter or margarine (1 stick),
   melted and cooled

1/2 cup more prepared coffee
1 (2-layer, 18.5-oz.) pkg. spice cake mix
1 cup chopped walnuts
1/2 cup semisweet chocolate chips

Preheat oven to 350°F (175°C). Butter a 13" x 9" baking pan; set aside. In a medium saucepan, combine caramels and 2 tablespoons coffee. Place over low heat until caramels melt; set aside. In a large bowl, combine melted butter or margarine, 1/2 cup coffee, cake mix and walnuts. Blend thoroughly. Spread half of batter evenly in prepared pan. Bake in preheated oven 10 minutes. Sprinkle chocolate chips over surface of hot cake. Drizzle caramel mixture over all. Top with remaining cake batter. Bake 20 minutes longer. When completely cooled, cut into about 2-1/2" x 1-1/2" bars. Makes 36 bars.

Coffee Toffee

The coffee lover's candy.

2 cups brown sugar, firmly packed
1/4 cup butter or margarine,
   room temperature
1 tablespoon vinegar

2 tablespoons water
Pinch salt
2 tablespoons instant coffee powder

Butter a shallow 13" x 9" baking pan; set aside. In a medium saucepan, combine brown sugar, butter or margarine, vinegar, water and salt. Stir to boiling. Boil without stirring to 290°F (143°C) on candy thermometer or soft-crack stage. Stir in instant coffee powder and pour immediately into prepared pan. Cool slightly. Mark into squares. When completely cool, break into pieces. Wrap pieces individually in wax paper, twisting ends, or wrap in aluminum foil. Makes about 24 candies.

Brazilian Truffles

A sophisticated sweet to serve with after-dinner coffee.

1 cup grated Brazil nuts
1 cup vanilla cookie wafer crumbs
1 (6-oz.) pkg. chocolate chips (1 cup)
1/2 cup granulated sugar

1/2 cup prepared coffee
1 tablespoon instant coffee powder
1/4 cup cocoa powder
1/2 cup powdered sugar

In a medium saucepan, combine Brazil nuts, cookie crumbs, chocolate chips, granulated sugar and coffee. Stir over low heat until sugar dissolves and chocolate melts. Cool to room temperature. Form into 3/4-inch balls. In a shallow bowl, mix instant coffee powder, cocoa and powdered sugar. Roll balls in mixture. Makes about 72 candies.

How To Make Date-Nut Log

1/Before making candy, line a baking sheet with aluminum foil. Sprinkle foil with powdered sugar. After candy has cooked, cooled and thickened, turn out onto prepared foil.

2/Divide candy in half. Shape each half into a 9-inch log. Roll in powdered sugar. Wrap in foil and refrigerate.

3/To serve, slice chilled log with a sharp knife dipped in hot water.

Date-Nut Log

Cut thick slices from the log and serve with steaming cups of coffee.

About 1/4 cup powdered sugar
4 cups granulated sugar
5 tablespoons butter or margarine,
  room temperature
1 cup water
1 (8-oz.) pkg. pitted dates, chopped

4 teaspoons instant coffee powder
1 tablespoon rum flavoring or
  1 teaspoon vanilla extract
1/2 cup finely chopped almonds or other nuts

Line a baking sheet or any flat surface with a double sheet of aluminum foil. Sprinkle with powdered sugar. In a large saucepan on high heat, combine sugar, butter or margarine and water. Cook to 234°F (112°C) on candy thermometer or soft-ball stage. Add chopped dates. Cook 2 to 3 minutes longer, blending dates into mixture. Remove from heat. Stir in instant coffee powder and rum flavoring or vanilla extract. Cool to lukewarm. Beat until candy begins to thicken. Add chopped nuts. Continue to beat until very thick and creamy. Turn candy out onto prepared aluminum foil. Form into two 9-inch logs. Roll in powdered sugar. Chill. To serve, slice into rounds with a sharp knife dipped in hot water. Makes 2 logs.

Pecan Brittle   *Photo on page 137.*

Everybody's favorite!

2 cups sugar
1 cup corn syrup
1/2 cup water
1 cup butter or margarine (2 sticks),
  room temperature

2 (6-oz.) pkgs. chopped pecans
2 tablespoons instant coffee powder
1 teaspoon baking soda

Generously butter 2 baking sheets with shallow sides. In a medium saucepan over low heat, blend sugar, corn syrup, water and butter or margarine. Cook to 250°F (121°C) on a candy thermometer or hard-ball stage. Stir in pecans and instant coffee powder. Cook to 280°F (138°C) or soft-crack stage. Remove from heat. Add baking soda; stir quickly until mixture foams. Pour immediately into prepared pans and spread thinly over entire surface. Cool until hard. Break into pieces. Makes about 2 pounds of candy.

Have you ever wondered what made your candy turn sugary instead of creamy smooth? The cause is formation of sugar crystals on the sides of the pan. You can prevent this by generously coating the entire inside of the pan with butter or margarine. The sugar crystals will still form, but they will slide back and melt into the candy.

Rocky Road Clusters

Fun to make and fun to eat!

1 (12-oz.) pkg. semisweet chocolate chips
   (2 cups)
2 tablespoons instant coffee powder
2 tablespoons butter or margarine,
   room temperature
1 tablespoon vegetable shortening,
   room temperature

1 cup raisins
2 cups miniature marshmallows
1 (8-oz.) jar unsalted dry roasted peanuts
   (1-1/2 cups), chopped

Line baking sheets or any flat surface with sheets of wax paper. Combine chocolate chips, instant coffee powder, butter or margarine and shortening in top of double boiler. Place over, not in, simmering water until chocolate melts; stir often to keep smooth. Remove from heat. Add remaining ingredients. Stir to blend. Drop by spoonfuls onto wax paper. Cool until firm. Makes about 36 candies.

Coffee Mints

Very delicately flavored.

1/4 cup sugar
2 tablespoons water
1/2 teaspoon peppermint extract
1/2 teaspoon cream of tartar

2 cups more sugar
6 tablespoons more water
1-1/2 tablespoons instant coffee powder

Line baking sheets or a flat surface with sheets of wax paper. Place 1/4 cup sugar, 2 tablespoons water, peppermint extract and cream of tartar in a small bowl. Blend well. In a medium saucepan, combine 2 cups sugar and 6 tablespoons water. Stir over medium heat until sugar dissolves and mixture comes to a full boil. Boil without stirring to 234°F (112°C) on candy thermometer or soft-ball stage. Stir in peppermint mixture. Remove from heat and beat with electric mixer on high speed until thick and creamy. Stir in instant coffee powder. Drop by half teaspoonfuls onto wax paper. When firm, peel mints from paper. Store in layers between wax paper in an airtight container. Makes about 72 candies.

Clockwise from top: Pecan Brittle, Coffee Mints, Rocky Road Clusters, Coffee Fudge.

Caramel-Nut Clusters

These disappear as fast as you make them.

1-1/2 cups caramel-coated
  popcorn and peanuts
1 (8-oz.) jar unsalted dry roasted peanuts
  (1-1/2 cups)
3 egg whites

1 cup sugar
1/4 cup all-purpose flour
2 tablespoons instant coffee powder

Butter baking sheets. Set aside. Preheat oven to 325°F (165°C). In a small bowl, mix caramel-coated popcorn and peanuts and dry roasted peanuts. In a large bowl, beat egg whites until soft peaks form when beaters are lifted from bowl. Add 8 tablespoons of the sugar 2 tablespoons at a time, beating after each addition. Continue to beat until mixture holds stiff peaks. Sift together remaining sugar, flour and instant coffee powder. Fold into egg white mixture. Fold in caramel-coated popcorn and peanut mixture. Drop by rounded teaspoonfuls onto prepared baking sheets. Bake in preheated oven 10 to 12 minutes. Cool on baking sheets 2 minutes. Cool completely on racks. Makes about 48 cookies.

If You Don't Have a Candy Thermometer:

Syrup has reached the soft-ball stage, 234° to 240°F (112° to 116°C), when about 1/4 teaspoon dropped into cold water can be shaped into a soft ball with your fingers. When you pick up the ball to remove it from the water, it falls apart.

Syrup has reached the hard-ball stage, 250° to 268°F (121° to 132°C), when about 1/4 teaspoon dropped into cold water can be shaped into a firm ball that is easily picked up.

Syrup has reached the soft-crack stage, 270° to 290°F (132° to 143°C), when about 1/4 teaspoon dropped into cold water separates into hard threads which can be picked up and bent.

Syrup has reached the hard-crack stage, 300° to 310°F (149° to 154°C), when about 1/4 teaspoon dropped into cold water forms brittle threads which remain brittle when removed from the water.

Coffee Fudge

Photo on page 137.

The best fudge you ever tasted!

2 cups light brown sugar, firmly packed	1/4 teaspoon salt
1 cup milk	3 tablespoons instant coffee powder
1/2 cup whipping cream	1 teaspoon vanilla extract
4 tablespoons light corn syrup	1 cup chopped pecans

Butter an 11" x 7" baking pan; set aside. Place brown sugar, milk, cream, corn syrup and salt in a medium saucepan. Stir over moderate heat until sugar dissolves. Continue to cook, stirring occasionally, to 234°F (112°C) on candy thermometer or soft-ball stage. Stir in instant coffee powder. Cool to lukewarm without stirring. Add vanilla extract. Beat until mixture thickens and is no longer glossy. Stir in pecans. Pour into prepared pan. Cut into about 1-1/2" x 1" pieces. Makes 42 candies.

Date Squares

Coffee subtly flavors the filling and the dough.

Coffee-Date Filling, see below	1/2 cup water
1 cup butter or margarine (2 sticks), melted	2 cups all-purpose flour
	1 teaspoon baking soda
1 cup brown sugar, firmly packed	1 cup oatmeal
1 tablespoon instant coffee powder	

Coffee-Date Filling:

1 (8-oz.) pkg. pitted dates, chopped	1 tablespoon instant coffee powder
1 cup sugar	1/2 cup chopped pecans
1/2 cup water	

Prepare Coffee-Date Filling; set aside. Preheat oven to 325°F (165°C). Generously oil a 12" x 8" baking pan; set aside. Combine melted butter or margarine, brown sugar, instant coffee powder and water in a large bowl. Blend well. Sift together flour and baking soda. Combine with oatmeal. Add to butter-sugar mixture. Beat well to blend. Spread half of dough over bottom of prepared pan. Cover with cooled Coffee-Date Filling. Spread remaining dough over filling. Bake in preheated oven 40 to 45 minutes. Cool to room temperature. Lift edges with spatula. Cut into 1-inch squares and place on rack to dry slightly. Makes 96 squares.

Coffee-Date Filling:
Combine all ingredients except pecans in a medium saucepan. Stir over medium heat until dates are very tender and filling is thick and smooth. Stir in pecans. Cool to room temperature.

Walnut Brownies

Chocolate brownies with a butter-coffee glaze.

1 cup cake flour
1/2 teaspoon baking powder
1/8 teaspoon baking soda
1/4 teaspoon salt
1/2 cup ground walnuts
1/2 cup butter or margarine (1 stick),
   room temperature

2 (1-oz.) squares unsweetened chocolate
1/2 cup prepared cold coffee
1 cup sugar
2 eggs, beaten
Butter Glaze, see below
1/4 cup more ground walnuts

Butter Glaze:
3 tablespoons butter or margarine
2 cups powdered sugar

1 to 2 tablespoons prepared cold coffee

Preheat oven to 350°F (175°C). Lightly oil a 12" x 8" baking pan. Line with wax paper. Butter the wax paper; set pan aside. Sift together flour, baking powder, baking soda and salt into a medium bowl. Stir in ground walnuts. Place butter or margarine and chocolate in a large saucepan over low heat until melted. Stir in coffee. Cool to room temperature. Stir in sugar. Add eggs. Blend well. Add to flour-nut mixture and blend thoroughly. Pour into prepared pan. Bake in preheated oven 30 minutes or until top springs back when lightly touched with fingertips. Cool in pan on rack. Prepare Butter Glaze. Spread over brownie surface. Sprinkle with 1/4 cup ground walnuts. Press walnuts into glaze. Cut into 2-inch squares and remove from pan with spatula. Makes 24 brownies.

Butter Glaze:
Cream butter or margarine in a small bowl until light and fluffy. Gradually beat in powdered sugar with 1 to 2 tablespoons cold coffee to bring to a spreadable consistency.

Praline Cookies

Crisp wafers flavored with coffee & pecans.

4 tablespoons butter or margarine,
   room temperature
1 cup light brown sugar, firmly packed
2 tablespoons instant coffee powder

1 egg, well beaten
1 cup flour
1 cup coarsely chopped pecans

Preheat oven to 350°F (175°C). Generously butter baking sheets; set aside. Melt butter or margarine over low heat. Combine in a medium bowl with brown sugar. Stir in instant coffee powder. Add egg. Blend well. Stir in flour and pecans. Drop onto prepared baking sheets by half teaspoonfuls about 1 inch apart. Bake in preheated oven 10 minutes. Loosen edges of cookies with a spatula. Cool on racks until crisp. Makes about 36 cookies.

Mocha Cookies

Crisp little wafers with an exotic flavor.

2 (1-oz.) squares unsweetened chocolate	1-1/2 cups sugar
2 tablespoons instant coffee powder	1 egg
1/4 cup water	1/4 teaspoon salt
1 teaspoon Angostura bitters	2-1/2 cups all-purpose flour
1/2 cup butter or margarine (1 stick), room temperature	2 teaspoons baking powder

Butter baking sheets; set aside. Combine chocolate, instant coffee powder and water in a small saucepan. Place over low heat until chocolate melts, stirring occasionally to keep smooth. Remove from heat and add bitters. Cool to room temperature. In a large bowl, cream butter or margarine with sugar. Add egg and beat well. Sift together salt, flour and baking powder. Add flour mixture to batter alternately with chocolate mixture. Blend thoroughly. Chill. Preheat oven to 350°F (175°C). On a lightly floured surface, roll out cold dough to 1/8-inch thick. Cut into shapes with small floured cookie cutters. Bake on prepared baking sheets in preheated oven 10 to 12 minutes. Makes about 48 cookies.

Dream Cookies

Serve fresh from the oven to enjoy the peak of their exquisite flavor.

1-1/2 cups cake flour	3/4 cup butter or margarine (1-1/2 sticks), room temperature
1 teaspoon baking powder	1 cup sugar
2 (1-oz.) squares unsweetened chocolate	1 egg
2 tablespoons instant coffee powder	2 tablespoons rum or 2 teaspoons rum flavoring
1/4 cup water	

Preheat oven to 350°F (175°C). Butter baking sheets; set aside. Sift together flour and baking powder. In a small saucepan combine chocolate, instant coffee powder and water. Place over low heat until chocolate melts. In a medium bowl, cream butter or margarine with sugar until light and fluffy. Add melted chocolate mixture, egg and rum or rum flavoring. Beat until well blended. Add flour mixture. Blend well. Drop by spoonfuls onto prepared baking sheets. Bake in preheated oven 8 to 10 minutes. Cool on racks. Makes about 48 cookies.

Let cookies cool only briefly on the baking sheet then place them on a rack to finish cooling. Otherwise they will continue to cook on the hot baking sheet. Let the baking sheet cool completely before recoating it with butter or margarine for the next batch.

Sandwich Cookies

Put these together in a jiffy.

1 cup butter or margarine (2 sticks),
   room temperature
1 cup sugar
2 egg yolks
1 tablespoon instant coffee powder

1 teaspoon vanilla extract
2 cups all-purpose flour
Raspberry or apricot jam
Powdered sugar

Preheat oven to 350°F (175°C). In a medium bowl, cream butter or margarine with sugar until very light and fluffy. Add egg yolks. Beat well. Stir in instant coffee powder and vanilla extract. Add flour. Stir to a stiff dough. Chill. When ready to bake, divide dough into 4 sections. Return 3 sections to the refrigerator. On a lightly floured surface, roll out fourth section to 1/8-inch thick. With floured cookie cutter, cut into rounds. Place on ungreased baking sheet. Bake in preheated oven 10 to 12 minutes until edges just begin to brown. Don't overbake. Cool completely. Repeat with remaining 3 sections of dough. Spread half of cookies with raspberry or apricot jam. Top with remaining cookies and press together sandwich-fashion. Dust with powdered sugar. Makes about 36 sandwich cookies.

Schoolhouse Raisin Cookies

Easy and economical—but so good!

1/3 cup raisins
3 tablespoons instant coffee powder
1-1/2 cups boiling water
1/2 cup butter or margarine (1 stick),
   room temperature

1 cup sugar
2 eggs
3-1/2 cups all-purpose flour

Combine raisins, instant coffee powder and boiling water. Stir until coffee dissolves. Set aside 2 to 3 hours. Cream butter or margarine with sugar in a large bowl until light and fluffy. Add eggs 1 at a time, beating well after each addition. Add raisin-coffee mixture. Blend well. Add flour about 1/3 cup at a time, beating well after each addition. Cover dough and refrigerate 1 to 2 hours. Dough wrapped in aluminum foil may be refrigerated 2 to 3 days, or frozen 2 to 3 weeks. Let thaw completely before making cookies. Preheat oven to 350°F (175°C). Lightly oil baking sheets. Drop batter by small teaspoons about 1-1/2 inches apart onto prepared baking sheets. Bake in preheated oven 15 to 20 minutes. Let cool slightly, then place on racks. Makes about 60 cookies.

Clockwise from top: Sandwich Cookies, Schoolhouse Raisin Cookies, Peanut Mixacookies and Black Pepper Cookies.

Peanut Mixacookies

Photo on page 143.

Coffee, peanuts and a cake mix make surprisingly good cookies!

2 tablespoons instant coffee powder
1/3 cup hot water
1 (18.5-oz.) pkg. yellow cake mix
2 eggs
1/4 cup butter or margarine (1/2 stick),
   room temperature

1 cup peanut butter, room temperature
1 (8-oz.) jar unsalted dry roasted peanuts,
   (1-1/2 cups), chopped

Butter baking sheets; set aside. Preheat oven to 350°F (175°C). Stir instant coffee powder into water. Cool. Place half of cake mix, eggs, butter or margarine, peanut butter and cooled coffee in a large bowl. Stir to blend, then beat until smooth. Stir in remaining cake mix and peanuts. Drop by spoonfuls, about 2 inches apart onto prepared baking sheets. Bake in preheated oven 10 to 12 minutes. Cool on rack. Makes about 72 cookies.

Black Pepper Cookies

Photo on page 143.

Delicate little cookies with just a touch of spice.

1 cup butter or margarine,
   room temperature
1-1/4 cups sugar
1 egg
2 (1-oz.) squares unsweetened chocolate

2 tablespoons instant coffee powder
3/4 cup water
2 cups all-purpose flour
1 teaspoon pepper
Pecan halves, if desired

In a large bowl, cream butter or margarine with sugar until light and fluffy. Add egg. Blend well. Combine chocolate, instant coffee powder and water in a small saucepan. Place over very low heat until chocolate is just melted. Cool 2 or 3 minutes. Stir into batter, blending well. Combine flour and pepper. Add to batter. Beat well to blend. Chill dough 1 to 2 hours, or longer if desired. Preheat oven to 350°F (175°C). Oil a baking sheet. Drop cookies by very small spoonfuls 1 inch apart onto baking sheet. If desired, press a pecan half on each cookie. Bake in preheated oven 10 to 12 minutes. Cool slightly on baking sheet. Cool completely on racks. Cookies keep well stored in a foil-lined tin box with tight-fitting lid. Makes about 72 cookies.

If there's too little cookie dough left to fill the last spaces in the baking sheet, crumple a small piece of aluminum foil and place it in the unused space. This will help the cookies bake and brown evenly.

Picture-Pretty Almond Cookies

Delectable mocha-glazed balls with a surprise inside each one!

3 cups all-purpose flour
1 teaspoon baking powder
1 tablespoon instant coffee powder
1/4 teaspoon salt
1 cup butter or margarine (1 stick),
    room temperature

1/2 cup light brown sugar, firmly packed
2 eggs
1/2 teaspoon almond extract
48 blanched almonds
Mocha Glaze, see below

Mocha Glaze:

1 (6-oz.) pkg. semisweet chocolate chips
    (1 cup)
1 tablespoon instant coffee powder

1 tablespoon light corn syrup
1 tablespoon milk
More milk if needed

Preheat oven to 350°F (175°C). Sift together flour, baking powder, instant coffee powder and salt. In a medium bowl, cream butter or margarine with brown sugar. Add eggs. Beat until very light and smooth. Stir in almond extract. Stir in flour mixture. Blend well. Refrigerate dough 1 to 2 hours. Shape into balls using about 1 tablespoon dough for each ball. Press 1 almond into each ball, covering it completely with dough. Place balls about 2 inches apart on an ungreased baking sheet. Bake in preheated oven 10 to 12 minutes or until cookies are done through center. Cool on racks. Prepare Mocha Glaze. With tongs, dip each cookie into hot glaze to coat tops. Let dry on rack. Makes about 48 cookies.

Mocha Glaze:
Combine chocolate chips, instant coffee powder and corn syrup in top of double boiler. Place over, not in, simmering water until chocolate melts. Stir in milk. Blend well. Keep warm over hot water. Add more milk if glaze becomes too thick.

Icebox Peanut Wafers

Make and freeze your own refrigerator cookies.

1 (8-oz.) jar unsalted dry roasted peanuts
    (1-1/2 cups)
1/2 cup butter or margarine (1 stick),
    room temperature

1 cup brown sugar, firmly packed
2 tablespoons instant coffee powder
1 tablespoon hot water
3/4 cup all-purpose flour

Place peanuts in blender container. Blend until pulverized. In a medium bowl, cream butter or margarine with brown sugar until light and fluffy. Dissolve instant coffee powder in hot water. Add dissolved coffee and peanuts to butter-sugar mixture. Add flour. Blend well. Chill dough until stiff enough to handle. Place on aluminum foil. Form into a 15-inch-long narrow roll and wrap in foil. Freeze. When ready to bake, preheat oven to 350°F (175°C). Generously butter baking sheets. Cut 1/4-inch slices and bake on prepared baking sheets 6 to 8 minutes. Do not overcook. Cool on racks. Makes about 60 cookies.

Raspberry Squares

Try one for breakfast!

2 cups all-purpose flour
1 teaspoon baking powder
1/4 teaspoon baking soda
1-3/4 cups quick-cooking oatmeal
1 cup brown sugar, firmly packed

1/4 cup instant coffee powder
3/4 cup butter or margarine (1-1/2 sticks),
   cut into small cubes
1 cup raspberry jam

Preheat oven to 350°F (175°C). Sift together flour, baking powder and baking soda into a medium bowl. Stir in oatmeal, brown sugar and instant coffee powder. With a pastry blender or 2 knives, cut in the butter or margarine until mixture resembles coarse crumbs. Place about 2/3 of mixture in an ungreased 11" x 7" baking dish. With fingers, press out evenly. Spread with raspberry jam. Cover evenly with remaining mixture. Press down lightly. Bake in preheated oven 30 to 35 minutes or until just lightly browned. Cool in pan. Cut into 1-3/4-inch squares. Makes 24 squares.

Viennese Crescents

Famous cookies from the coffee houses of old Vienna.

1 teaspoon vanilla extract
1 cup sugar
6 (1-oz.) squares semisweet chocolate
2 tablespoons instant coffee powder
2 cups all-purpose flour
1/4 cup butter or margarine (1/2 stick),
   room temperature

2 eggs, well beaten
1 cup more sugar
1 teaspoon grated lemon peel
1 egg white, slightly beaten

Stir vanilla extract into 1 cup sugar. Cover and let stand overnight. Shave chocolate with a small sharp kitchen knife. In a small bowl, combine chocolate shavings with instant coffee powder. Place flour in a large bowl. With pastry blender or 2 knives, blend butter or margarine into flour until mixture resembles cornmeal. Add eggs, 1 cup sugar, chocolate-coffee mixture and lemon peel. Blend well. Chill dough. Preheat oven to 350°F (175°C). Lightly butter baking sheets; set aside. On a lightly floured surface, roll out dough to 1/8-inch thick. Cut into shapes with floured crescent-shaped cookie cutter. Place on prepared baking sheets. Brush with beaten egg white. Sprinkle with vanilla-sugar mixture. Bake in preheated oven 10 minutes. Makes about 144 cookies.

1/Cut cubes of butter or margarine into flour-oatmeal mixture until mixture resembles coarse crumbs.

2/Press about 2/3 of mixture into an ungreased baking dish.

How To Make Raspberry Squares

3/Cover with a layer of raspberry jam. Top with remaining flour-oatmeal mixture. With back of spoon, press down lightly.

4/Bake until lightly browned. Cool and cut into squares.

Crisp Gingersnaps

You'll be pleased with the success of this homemade version.

2-1/2 cups all-purpose flour
1/4 teaspoon baking soda
1/2 teaspoon mixed apple pie spice
1/8 teaspoon salt
1/2 cup molasses

4 tablespoons instant coffee powder
1/2 cup butter or margarine (1 stick),
   room temperature
1/2 cup sugar
1 egg, slightly beaten

Preheat oven to 350°F (175°C). Butter baking sheets; set aside. Sift together flour, baking soda, apple pie spice and salt into a medium bowl. Place molasses in a small saucepan. Stir in instant coffee powder. Add butter or margarine. Stir over low heat until melted. Stir in sugar. Cool to lukewarm. Add beaten egg; blend well. Pour over flour mixture. Stir to a smooth dough. Chill. Divide into 4 sections. On a lightly floured surface, roll out a section at a time to 1/8-inch thick. With a floured cookie cutter, cut into small rounds. Place on prepared baking sheets. Bake in preheated oven 10 to 15 minutes. Cool on racks. Makes about 48 cookies.

Almond Fingers

Dainty cookie fingers to serve with ice cream.

1/4 cup sugar
3/4 cup very finely chopped slivered almonds
2 tablespoons instant coffee powder
1/2 cup butter or margarine (1 stick)

3/4 cup more sugar
2 eggs
2 cups all-purpose flour
1 egg, beaten

Combine 1/4 cup sugar, 3 tablespoons of the almonds and instant coffee powder; set aside. Cream butter or margarine with 3/4 cup sugar. Add 2 eggs. Beat until light and fluffy. Add remaining almonds and flour. Blend to a stiff dough. Chill well. Preheat oven to 350°F (175°C). Lightly butter baking sheets. Divide dough into thirds. On a lightly floured surface, roll out dough a third at a time to 1/8 inch thick. Cut into finger-length strips about 1/2 inch wide. Place on prepared baking sheets. Brush with egg. Sprinkle with sugar, almond and coffee mixture. Bake in preheated oven 10 to 12 minutes or until lightly browned. Makes about 96 cookies.

Spirited Coffees

Classic after-dinner coffees such as Café Royale and Irish Coffee begin this unusual group of recipes. Serve these coffees instead of, with or after dessert. In fact, some are desserts in themselves.

Café Brûlot or Café au Diable was a popular after-dinner drink in New Orleans during the Victorian era. For most of us it's too much trouble, but Café Brûlot is still served in some sophisticated restaurants. Part of its appeal is in watching the preparations. If you have enough confidence to tackle it, go ahead: Pour 2 to 4 demitasse cups of brandy—1 for each serving—into a chafing dish. Drop in a thin slice of orange and another of lemon, 4 to 6 cubes of sugar and 2 to 3 whole cloves. Heat over a low flame. When steaming hot, carefully ignite the brandy and let it flame briefly. Put out the flame by pouring over it an amount of hot coffee equal to the amount of flaming brandy. Ladle immediately into demitasse cups.

At my house I often end a dinner with spirited coffee and a make-ahead dessert like cookies or candy. See the recipes for Cookies & Candies, pages 132 to 148, for some of the most fabulous desserts you can imagine! Although it's an easy way out for you, spirited coffee served wtih a tray of cookies and candies is a distinctive and delicious enough dessert for your most important guests.

The chilled party specials you'll also find in this section will bring you fame as an innovative party-giver. Coffee Eggnog is an elegant and different drink to make your tree trimming party a gala event. Mocha Mint is a lovely blend of coffee, chocolate ice cream and crème de menthe, garnished with a delicate mint wafer.

This book would not be complete without it's final recipe—a delicious coffee liqueur. Make it for special at-home evenings or give it proudly to a favored friend.

Holiday Dessert Buffet

Louisiana Brandied Fruitcake, page 103
Java Spice Cake, page 93
Dobos Torte, page 96
Mincemeat Squares, page 102
Coffee Eggnog, page 155
Cafè á l'Orange, page 152

Café Royale

A New Orleans after-dinner classic.

Enough prepared hot coffee to fill coffee
   cup to within 1/2 inch of rim
1 tablespoon warm brandy

1 small sugar cube
About 1 teaspoon more warm brandy

Fill a demitasse or small cup to within 1/2 inch of rim with hot coffee. Gently pour 1 tablespoon of warm brandy over surface. Do not stir; brandy should float on top of coffee. Place sugar in coffee spoon. Fill spoon with warm brandy. Ignite brandy in spoon. As brandy flames, lower spoon gently into cup, igniting the brandy on surface of coffee. Stir until flame burns out. Makes 1 serving.

Mocha Mint

An exquisite dessert or drink.

1 cup prepared coffee
1 pint chocolate ice cream

1/4 cup crème de menthe
Very thin chocolate-mint wafers

Combine coffee, ice cream and crème de menthe in blender container. Blend on low speed. Spoon into sherbet or wine glasses. Garnish each serving with a chocolate mint wafer. Makes 4 servings.

Sassy Sodas

Delightful sipping!

1 pint coffee ice cream
2 tablespoons instant coffee powder
1/2 cup light rum

4 to 6 small scoops vanilla ice cream
Instant coffee powder for garnish

Spoon coffee ice cream into blender container. Add 2 tablespoons instant coffee powder and rum. Blend on high speed until creamy smooth. Pour into 4 to 6 tall glasses. Add a scoop of vanilla ice cream to each glass. Sprinkle lightly with instant coffee powder. Serve with long-handled spoons and soda straws. Makes 4 to 6 servings.

Irish Coffee

The idea is to sip hot coffee through chilled heavy cream.

6 tablespoons whipping cream
4 small sugar cubes

1/2 cup Irish whiskey
3 cups prepared hot coffee

Whip cream until thickened but not stiff. Chill. Preheat 4 Irish Coffee glasses, thick glasses with stems or heavy mugs by rinsing in hot water. Dry thoroughly. Place 1 sugar cube and 2 tablespoons whiskey in each glass. Crush sugar cube with the back of a spoon. Add 3/4 cup hot coffee to each glass. Slowly pour thickened cream over back of spoon on top of coffee, filling glass to brim; do not stir. Makes 4 servings.

How To Make Irish Coffee

1/Place sugar cube and whiskey in glass. With the back of a teaspoon, crush sugar cube against side of glass.

2/Pour coffee into glass. Pour thickened cream over back of spoon so it gently spreads over top of coffee. Do not stir. Cream should float on surface of coffee.

Café à l'Orange

The zest of orange with the richness of coffee.

1/2 cup whipping cream
2 tablespoons powdered sugar
1 teaspoon grated orange peel
3 cups prepared hot coffee

1/2 cup Grand Marnier liqueur or
   other orange liqueur
1 orange slice, cut in 4 wedges

In a small bowl, beat cream until stiff. Fold in powdered sugar and grated orange peel. Chill. Pour hot coffee equally into 4 coffee cups. Stir 2 tablespoons liqueur into each cup. Top with chilled whipped cream. Garnish with an orange wedge. Makes 4 servings.

Viennese Special

Forget the calories and just enjoy it!

1/2 cup whipping cream
1 egg white
2 tablespoons sugar

4 tablespoons brandy
2 cups prepared hot coffee
Cinnamon

In a small bowl, beat cream until stiff. In another small bowl, beat egg white until frothy. Add sugar 1 tablespoon at a time, beating after each addition. Continue to beat until shiny peaks form when beaters are lifted from bowl. Fold into whipped cream. Spoon equally into 4 mugs or cups. Combine brandy and coffee. Pour into mugs or cups over whipped cream mixture. Lightly sprinkle each serving with cinnamon. Makes 4 servings.

Brandied Chocolate Punch

Put leftover breakfast coffee in ice cube trays for an afternoon coffee refresher.

1 cup prepared cold coffee
1 cup milk

2 squares semisweet chocolate, melted
2 tablespoons brandy

Freeze coffee in ice cube tray. Combine frozen cubes with milk, chocolate and brandy in blender container. Blend until frothy. Serve at once. Makes 2 servings.

Irish Coffee on the Rocks

Always be prepared with 1 or 2 trays of coffee ice cubes in the freezer.

2 cups prepared cold coffee
1/2 cup whipping cream
8 tablespoons sugar

2 cups prepared hot coffee
1/2 cup Irish whiskey

Freeze cold coffee in ice cube trays. Whip cream until stiff. Chill. Place 2 tablespoons sugar in each of 4 tall glasses. Place long-handled spoons in glasses. Add 1/2 cup hot coffee to each glass. Stir until sugar dissolves. Add 2 tablespoons whiskey to each glass. Blend well. Fill glasses with coffee ice cubes. Top with chilled whipped cream. Makes 4 servings.

Crème de Cáfe

Crème de menthe and hot coffee blend in a beautiful after-dinner drink.

1/4 cup Alice Hasting's Coffee Liqueur,
   page 156, or other coffee liqueur
1/4 cup white crème de menthe

1-1/2 cups prepared hot coffee
About 4 tablespoons whipped cream
Shaved semisweet chocolate for garnish

Combine coffee liqueur and crème de menthe. Pour equally into two 8-ounce mugs. Fill each with hot coffee. Top each with about 2 tablespoons whipped cream. Sprinkle with shaved semisweet chocolate. Makes 2 servings.

Cappucino Cooler

The sophisticated milkshake.

2 tablespoons instant espresso
   coffee powder
2 tablespoons hot water
1 cup milk

2 small scoops coffee ice cream
1/4 cup brandy or bourbon
Dash vanilla extract
Nutmeg

In a small bowl, stir instant coffee powder into hot water. Add milk. Blend well. Pour into blender container. Add ice cream, brandy or bourbon and vanilla extract. Blend until smooth and frothy. Pour into 2 tall glasses. Sprinkle with nutmeg. Serve immediately. Makes 2 servings.

Monte Carlo

This spectacular coffee is really an exquisite dessert!

1/4 cup whipping cream
2 teaspoons warmed Cognac or
   other fine brandy
4 teaspoons sugar
1/2 cup more warmed Cognac or
   other fine bandy
2 cups freshly made, hot coffee

1/2 pint vanilla ice cream
1/4 cup Alice Hasting's Coffee Liqueur,
    page 156, or other coffee liqueur
2 tablespoons green crème de menthe
Instant coffee powder or espresso
   powder for garnish

Whip cream until stiff. Chill. Rinse 4 Irish Coffee glasses or heavy glasses with stems in very hot water. Dry thoroughly. Pour about 1/2 teaspoon warmed brandy into each. Swirl glasses to moisten insides with brandy. Add a teaspoon of sugar to each glass and rotate glasses to coat insides evenly. Prepare drinks 1 at a time: Pour 2 tablespoons warmed brandy into glass. Ignite with a long match. Rotate glass until flame burns out. Half fill with hot coffee. Add 3 to 4 heaping tablespoons ice cream. Pour in about 1 tablespoon coffee liqueur. Top with chilled whipped cream. Slowly pour a little crème de menthe over whipped cream. Sprinkle with instant coffee powder or espresso powder and serve at once. Makes 4 servings.

Coffee Eggnog

Make it once and they'll expect you to make it every year!

8 eggs, separated
1 cup sugar
3/4 cup bourbon

3/4 cup prepared cold coffee
1/2 cup whipping cream
Nutmeg

Combine egg yolks and sugar in top of double boiler. Place over, not in, simmering water and beat with electric or rotary beater until very light and fluffy. Remove from heat and continue to beat until mixture cools to room temperature. Stir in bourbon and coffee. In a large bowl, beat cream until stiff. Fold in egg yolk mixture. Refrigerate. Just before serving, beat egg whites until stiff. Fold into eggnog. Serve in goblets or mugs. Sprinkle each serving with nutmeg. Makes 8 to 12 servings.

Café Crème de Cacao

Coffee with a twist!

2 teaspoons sugar
1/2 cup prepared hot coffee
1/4 cup crème de cacao

1/4 cup Cognac or other fine brandy
1 thin lemon peel sliver

Place sugar in an 8-ounce mug. Pour hot coffee over sugar. Stir until sugar dissolves. Add crème de cacao and Cognac or other brandy. Twist lemon peel sliver over drink to extract oil essence. Drop peel into mug. Makes 1 serving.

Alice Hasting's Coffee Liqueur

Make your own after-dinner liqueur.

4 cups sugar
1/2 cup instant coffee powder
3 cups water

1/4 teaspoon salt
2-1/2 cups 80 proof vodka
1 tablespoon vanilla extract

In a large saucepan, combine sugar, instant coffee powder, water and salt. Stir over low heat until sugar and coffee dissolve. Bring to a full boil. Reduce heat; barely simmer 30 minutes. Remove from heat. Add vodka and vanilla extract. Blend well. Cool. Fill canning or freezing jars about 3/4 full. Seal. Store in refrigerator or freezer. Makes about 1-1/2 quarts.

Index

CONVERSION TO METRIC MEASURE

WHEN YOU KNOW	SYMBOL	MULTIPLY BY	TO FIND	SYMBOL
teaspoons	tsp	5	milliliters	ml
tablespoons	tbsp	15	milliliters	ml
fluid ounces	fl oz	30	milliliters	ml
cups	c	0.24	liters	l
pints	pt	0.47	liters	l
quarts	qt	0.95	liters	1
ounces	oz	28	grams	g
pounds	lb	0.45	kilograms	kg
Fahrenheit	°F	5/9 (after subtracting 32)	Celsius	C
inches	in	2.54	centimeters	cm
feet	ft	30.5	centimeters	cm

LIQUID MEASURE TO MILLILITERS

1/4 teaspoon	=	1.25 milliliters
1/2 teaspoon	=	2.5 milliliters
3/4 teaspoon	=	3.75 milliliters
1 teaspoon	=	5 milliliters
1-1/4 teaspoons	=	6.25 milliliters
1-1/2 teaspoons	=	7.5 milliliters
1-3/4 teaspoons	=	8.75 milliliters
2 teaspoons	=	10 milliliters
1 tablespoon	=	15 milliliters
2 tablespoons	=	30 milliliters

LIQUID MEASURE TO LITERS

1/4 cup	=	0.06 liters
1/2 cup	=	0.12 liters
3/4 cup	=	0.18 liters
1 cup	=	0.24 liters
1-1/4 cups	=	0.3 liters
1-1/2 cups	=	0.36 liters
2 cups	=	0.48 liters
2-1/2 cups	=	0.6 liters
3 cups	=	0.72 liters
3-1/2 cups	=	0.84 liters
4 cups	=	0.96 liters
4-1/2 cups	=	1.08 liters
5 cups	=	1.2 liters
5-1/2 cups	=	1.32 liters

FAHRENHEIT TO CELSIUS

F	C
200°	95°
225°	110°
250°	120°
275°	135°
300°	150°
325°	165°
350°	180°
375°	190°
400°	205°
425°	220°
450°	230°
475°	245°
500°	260°

11.05128887891